DOWNWIND
FROM NOBODY

Joan Wells

GARDEN WAY PUBLISHING
CHARLOTTE · VERMONT 05445

To Mike,
whose strength supports a mountain.
That mountain supports me.

Illustrations by Sherry Streeter
Printed in the United States
Second Printing, November 1978

Library of Congress Cataloging in Publication Data
Well, Joan, 1927–
  Downwind from nobody.

  1. Country life—Oregon. 2. Wells, Joan,
1927– I. Title.
S521.5.07W44   979.5   78-14882
ISBN 0-88266-144-2

Contents

II

I COULD TURN
AND LIVE WITH THE ANIMALS

III

WHAT SHALL I LEARN OF THE BEANS?

IV

BEYOND SUBSISTENCE

Acknowledgments

The Craft That Built These Holes So True," reprinted by permission from *Blair & Ketchum's Country Journal*. Copyright © 1977, Country Journal Publishing Company, Brattleboro, Vermont. "Reverence for Life . . ." reprinted by permission of *Harrowsmith Magazine*, Camden East, Ontario, KOK, 1JO. "To Husband a Goat . . ." and "Happy in Hendom" reprinted by permission of *Farmstead*, Freedom, ME. Several of Apostrophes reprinted by permission of *Times-Journal*, Condon, OR.

Preface

It's one hundred-sixty acres of woods sitting astride a gentle mountain. Near its middle is a meadow furnished with wild grasses and gnarled apple trees. Above the old orchard, the ground levels before climbing again, and on that flat space our home cabin rests. From its kitchen window we can look past the pear thicket and the hillside garden, down to the valley's cleavage and to the ranges beyond, marching as far as the eye can see. But for the one valley farm we can view from our hillside, we might be sole survivors of a world only dimly remembered.

"There's an old shack up there you'll probably want to tear down," said the realtor describing this piece of land. When we found it, examined its weathered boards, picked apples from its front porch and sat very still in its quiet shadows, we translated his words into blasphemy. Weather-beaten, battered, leaking and creaky though it might be, this cabin had the rare feel of HOME. Neither of us had to say it; we simply set our minds to how we'd repair it, make it weather-worthy, make ourselves worthy of its having stood and waited for so many years.

The tall-boarded cabin now has a kitchen attached to it, built with our blood, sweat and sinew two years back. Next to the old log shed, Mike's workshop rises, and between it and the cabin there's the patched-up greenhouse whose walls the goats ate one year. Scattered across the hillside below are the outhouse and root cellar, the chicken coop and goat barn.

Sometimes when I climb the meadow and look at our buildings' spread, I feel sad that we've tamed it so, that it couldn't have been left to its nature, overgrown and serene. There are other times, when summer visitors crowd our grounds, or when heavy weathers keep the goats in their minuscule barn, that I wish for structures enough to satisfy each creature comfort. But the goats don't seem to notice the size of their shelter, and two rooms with a sleeping loft under the sky are all two people need, if they're friends. And one-hundred-sixty acres of woods, creek, meadow and hollow are more than enough to absorb and examine and learn by heart in anyone's earthly lifetime.

Introduction

Though there is always a raft of questions, no one ever asks why. Why we fled one of the finest coastal cities to settle into an untamed mountain farm, gave up city jobs and pleasures to hard-scrabble in a sparsely settled spread of rough land. It's a good thing they don't, really. Our answers might take a book, would prompt at least a whole mess of chapters.

How? That is the question asked most of the time, usually by city folk, with equal parts of envy and awe. How we green city dwellers learned country ways, how we survive without salaries or urban sophistications; how we entertain ourselves, maintain our sanity in deep solitude, raise animals and crops we had known next to nothing about.

Though we've a legion of becauses available, the hows are harder to answer. We are still exploring the ways. If we weren't, if there were no surprise and challenge, there would be little reason to stay.

I find myself wishing sometimes that all the freshman farmers who have fled their generation's cities to live with and from the land could hold annual meetings wherein they could share their unique country ways. We might even agree to let in a few city dwellers for old time's sake. What tall tales we'd tell about our successes and pratfalls, what banter we'd build over garden and kitchen deeds and farm creature care.

Sadly, such a meeting isn't likely. No tiller of soil or caretaker of stock could get away to take part. We're all too busy about our rows of beans, with treating poor Bessie's bloat or mending fences, or patching up rig, roof or beast. Farm-bound, which, given the choices, is a singularly reasonable condition in which to be.

Mike and I have been farmers for seven years now. Having come to it late, we tasted more of urban living and delved further into city alternatives than most of our emigrant-kin. We suspect this gives us an advantage, an awareness of the exchange. We did not, in honesty, see clearly all we would gain.

"Are you glad you did it?" the outsider asks.

"Yes, absolutely."

"You're happy here?"

"Yes, most of the time, and at peace."

"Would you do it over?"

"Yes, positively."

"Would you do it the same?"

A pause there. Maybe. Give me a minute. That's one I need to ponder, take time to fathom. We are nearing the depths.

I

IT TAKES

A HEAP O' LIVIN'

Back to Whose Land?

Searching, restless, always on the move, that's the way of most urban survivors. In their upward, outward, everward mobility, they're in constant quest for a nicer apartment, a roomier home, a more private patch of green for their play. But when one chooses a spread in the country, it will likely be a permanent shelter, a place where roots will be planted and a patch of soil becomes part of one's very being. If anything in life demands wisdom and study, it is that search and selection.

"Oh, wow, far out!" one young seeker exploded for three consecutive days upon reaching our hilltop. "What a neat root cellar, far out! "What a groovy outhouse, too much!" "That spring tank is outta sight!"

He had left a big eastern city weeks earlier with a $2000 stash to find a place in our state where he could, in the common lingo, Live Off the Land.

"Whose land?" we asked, as gently as we knew how.

"I'll find it. That's what the $2000's for."

"You'll need more, and then more, to settle."

"Don't worry, it's cool. I'm an artist. I can sell my paintings, maybe sketch some old barns for barter."

Where would he find time and energy to sketch, after building, mending, gardening and cutting wood, harvesting and raising critters, mending, and mending. . . ? No, we didn't ask that, though I wish now we had. He came to us for help and we were too easy. If we'd been more gut-level honest, he might not have failed, might not have been driven back to the city with dead dreams and empty jeans.

Though there is no one right way to do it, there are as many wrong directions to rural simplicity as there are first-time-farmer failures. Having watched more than our share, a few dear friends among them, I want to try to be gut-level honest, even with myself, which is hardest of all.

It's every other city dweller's dream these days to live in some pastoral haven, to escape urban clamor, pollution and the crimes crowdedness breeds; to become master of one's own schedule and deprogram oneself from imposed city routines. Further, the fantasy model often boasts visions of fields dotted with bovines, cock-crow for alarm, woodstoves crackling while snow drifts past a hand-built cabin window. Such visions can be made reality; such visions only skim the panorama country life means.

For starters, those grazing bovines must be fenced and housed, and fences and structures demand time and money. And the cows have to be fed, and feed means planting and nurturing and harvesting their provender, which requires an investment in a clutch of pretty-penny farm equipment. If you want milk from your charges, you must forfeit your dreams of living outside of schedules and imposed routines. Whereas in the city you can run to the corner market for a carton of potables, on a functioning farm you must appear in the barn with your bucket each morning and eve, whether you've busted your arm or Gabriel has sounded his clarion. And the cocks won't be there to crow nor will the hens bring forth their eggs if you don't feed and water them daily and lock them up nightly against an array of wily thieves. And the eggs won't taste right if you don't gather them fresh

(twice a day in hot weather), and the home-grown Kentucky
Colonel won't be succulent if you don't butcher in proper
season. As for the crackling wood stove and the Christmas
card visions of snow, there's a trade for those too. The logs
must be cut, hauled, chopped (assuming, of course, one has
the required equipment), seasoned and sheltered. If you
cherish your farmhouse's safety, the chimney must be kept
free of sclerosis and the stove's innards maintained in good
shape.

That done, it is then lovely to settle down and rock by the
fire, sated with worthy chores (rest well, for they'll be there
tomorrow) and watch the snow sift by the panes . . . ignoring
the crack where the cold seeps which you haven't found
time yet to mend. Lovely, that is, if a snowplow is handy or
the road crew is minding its business, or if you welcome your
solitude and don't mind being out of touch with the postbox,

much less the nearest town for a spell, or the likelihood that the lines will topple and the power will fail and the telephone be out of commission for days without measure. And then there's that leak in the barn roof you've been meaning to fix, and the path to the coop will need shoveling out before breakfast, and if the logs aren't crackling merrily, it's probably that green wood you didn't get chopped or seasoned on time because the calf took sick in early summer and the cows breached the fence and the spring tank sprung a leak in its nethers.

As I said, those are starters, a sampling of rural simplicity once you've searched out and settled into your brave new pastoral world. Which takes me back to the selection part.

There is, I've found, an unbridgeable distance between escape and determined direction, a difference which has much to do with down-and-out failure and some semblance of making it. While escape is easy and ever at hand for the impatient or gypsy-souled, direction takes study, forbearance for detours, and a quality seldom mentioned in escapees' tragic tales: self-knowledge.

The first thing the country-bent planner should ask himself is WHY. If he is unhappy in a city or suburb, it would be wise to probe whether it's the fault of environment, or his own imperfect spirit. For it is guaranteed that though the site can be metamorphozed, the all-too-familiar spirit will tag as doggedly as one's shadow. If it is a couple or family which is resettling, such a drastic change in life-style might well compound the hazards.

To avoid massive culture shock, the farmer-to-be should sit down with a balance sheet and list those items which nurture his unique hungers. How much does his social life count? What sorts of entertainment are vital? How much wit and wisdom beyond his own creativity does he require to hold off mental atrophy? How important is the daily paper, mobility, and time off for play? Farming, on any scale, is a hard task-master. You cannot tell the crops, flocks and stock that you're tired, you need a weekend of rest or a spell at the shore for diversion. And though you're bound to make new friends among neighbors and fellow farmers, they aren't likely to be conversant with the minutiae of worldly affairs or state of the arts. Discussions of crops or scours and the menu for the Grange picnic, though rich with rusticity, can soon starve a mind used to more intellectual fare. The "simple life" doesn't mean easy-going, which farming isn't; it signifies basic, un-adorned, bare.

Okay, say you feel in your bones you could forfeit the daily paper and social sophistications, are ready even to trade the city mill-treading for a passel of country chores. You are now free to fill the other side of the ledger with those dreams of pure air, wholesome victuals, kinship with nature, self-reli-ance. Which brings you to where the best place might be to avail yourself of such alchemy.

There is a raft of books on the market concerning the "best" places in this land to settle. Most of them read like a travel agent's tall tale, highlighting areas where the sun al-ways shines and the schools are top drawer and crime in the streets is unheard of. If someone suggested to *me* that those were the sole elements of the good life, I'd give him An-drew Marvell, "The grave's a fine and quiet place," and flee from his short-sighted view. Though there is probably not a soul on this earth who doesn't harbor a penchant for sunshine and the felicity of bonny weather, if a clement clime is near the top of your list, you had best prepare to pay well for your preference and to share it with hordes of like-souled sun-seekers. On the other hand, there are those gallants who thrive on the challenge of weathers and the march of mutable seasons, on the old gold autumn wears and the green promise spring sustains and those Christmas card winters when being pares down to the bone. Whatever one's prediliction, it is wise to be aware of it and to reckon what one wants to sacrifice in its name before pinning his hopes on a map full of unknowns.

Ideally, the way to test a rural location is to spend a good span of time in its bounds before commitment, to give oneself a chance to measure the weathers and mingle with neighbors and knock around nearby towns. This would give the future settler a chance to plumb whether the natives are the sort he can hunker down with and who might lend a hand in a pinch, if the creatures he means to take on are available and the supplies he'll need within convenient reach. (It being the first principle of farming that tools break and implements fail when you most sorely need them, a round trip of one hundred miles for their mending or replacement could be the final straw.) He could also explore the availability of medical and dental care, measure the schools' teaching and student transport, and find out about such vital concerns as easements for power and phone lines and roads and the habits of one's potential neighbors. (Is the farmer a few fences over hooked on chemical sprays, or does ol' Roy down the road let his fences collapse and his stock meander?) And what of the market for the wares he hopes to sell for his subsistence wages? There are counties on counties, I guarantee, which would starve out a da Vinci or Burbank in their set-minded midst.

Finally, it would be of no small consequence to weigh the culture of one's future homeland. For beyond the labor and learning, the breaking of earth and communion with her resources, the folks settled there, from the good ol' boys and town gossips to lawmen and shopkeepers, will be one's human resource for tapping and the social solace of one's infinite days. In balance, this human component might be the most telling of all. Inclement weathers, farm tribulations, incapacity even, are more easily borne when shared with friends and samaritans; successes and joys are highlighted by fellowship's celebration. In the city there exist work and play, co-workers and social companions. On a farm, they are one and the same, and if his farm kith are less than compatible, the new settler is likely to spend his days as an island, which few can contentedly be.

Remember, I said *ideally*. Again, each person's choice will rest in the end on his private, determined priorities. If one man's bliss rests in the view of the sunrise on his hill or a waterhole perfect for fishing or a thicket rife with wild creatures, he may willingly sacrifice more practical considerations. Who cares if supplies are a half-day away or the town council balks at maintaining his road, as long as deer peer through his windows and wild geese favor his pond? And what little matter if his bees perish of drifting poisons if there's a theatre workshop in town, or the neighbors have pined all along for his unique talents? Balance is just what it says: you take away here and put there until the scales level. If the fulfillments outweigh the deficiencies, you've chosen well.

Now, the gut-level honesty. We, Mike and I, managed but a few of the listed suggestions. We bought our acres after a single overnight visit because the land spoke to us and our initials were carved in the cabinside apple tree. We took the crewmaster's word for gospel that our road would be repaired and maintained for accessibility to our postbox and the down-mountain village. We assumed if we paid the price and contributed labor we could, in good time, electrify our humble holdings. Though we knew the nearest supplies and a medical center were fifty miles distant, knew even that the townfolk were suspicious of city slickers, we selected our cabin-crowned meadow and haven of pines in the bat of an eyelash. It had springs and a homesteader shack and a view next to heaven's. What more could a city-sick, peace-hungry couple ask?

Priorities. They're not simple to measure, are as precarious as man's moods and earth's seasons. It took us well past a year to settle an easement battle over the placement of power poles. After that, planting the phone line was but a piddling skirmish. For three years we waited and pleaded that the county road leading up to our meadow be made passable, three years of being landlocked over winter and during fall rains and spring thaws; three years of frequent and total isolation from the small world of supplies and mail delivery and doctors' care when we took, beyond home healing, sick. State law settled that struggle, but the county snowplow still disdains our weather-bound route. It's something to do with the crew-master's kin and suspicion of city slickers and Mike's beard and our uppity tongues. . . .

We're country miles past the ledger sheet now, past the weighing and looking for balance. Our initials in the old apple tree are more deeply etched, and its roots have us bound. The goats know their play yards by heart, the herb garden has weathered deer hungers, and the cocks crow up each dawn as though it were the first light of heaven.

If we had done it with studied foresight, as we now caution others, would our path have been easier? Probably. Given these seven years' wisdom, would we do it again, the same way? In deepest honesty, it's hard to say. It's been more blasted work than we'd ever envisioned, work smudged with that bane of routine. It's been lonely often; long-term isolation has plunged us into our deepest resources and we've at times scraped the barrel. But we live with the animals, are blessed with peace and earth's plenty. That world out there beyond our meadow and pines is alien now, though still somehow exotic. I guess, like all first-time farmers, we've a long way to go. Our direction feels unmistaken.

APOSTROPHE I

Vagrant May

A May day, and the last blossoms drift from the old apple trees, dressing the hillside with pale confetti. The dipping sun grazes the meadow, the meadow birds swoop in its spill like flitting shadows. The lark tucks silence about her, the dove mourn falls still.

Then dusk, and the farm familiars take on new shapes. The sage hunches, the young pine becomes a candelabrum, its whorls votives to heaven. Roosting chickens cluck gutteral lullabyes from their quarters, and the first evening star pulses over the chimney.

(In the city, they're most of them home now, putting cars into garages, switching TV dials to distract the day's trials.)

Dark now, and the owl in the east wood tunes up his crooning. His hesitant notes drift over the meadow, seeking an echo. It comes, a soft querulous whoo, from a branch by the uphill spring. I open the door to listen and breathe a prayer that the owls will meet under the moon in a soft mingling of answers.

Deeper night, the moon high. The cabin lights seep out the windows, making steep shadows in the dooryard. Beyond

them, the dogs race toward a gathering of eyes at the woods'
edge. The eyes disappear, taking their secrets into the secret
dark.

(In the city, they're switching off the night shows, check-
ing door locks, shutting windows to the growl of traffic and
the yowl of yard dogs who yearn to run under the moon. No
owl will soothe restless dreams, no cockcrow awaken.)

Before bedtime, I walk out under the sky. The hillside is
still but for the whisper of leaves and night's stirring stealth.
A star tumbles, and I wonder who in the world, watching,
stops his breath with mine.

(The city's loom dulls all but the brightest performer, the
city's maps are street-bound; mine probe the edge of infinity.)

Morning. The roosters announce the news and tug my
waking dream. Outside the bedside window, my eye catches
a flurry of white. Tag-end apple blossoms, harried by a morning breeze? No, that's . . . *snow!* On the day I was primed to
plant the peas, to toss winter boots into a cobwebbed closet.
A sullen light spreads over the room, and for morning prayer,
I curse the Judas season.

(In the city, tires hiss over the rainwet streets. Umbrellas
bob, vying for space, puddle sloshers dart for buildings'
shelter. Rainy days are fun among the multitude, bring people into a sort of damp communion. On our hill, it is snow,
and breached garden dreams.)

The chickens, huddled forlornly under trees, shake flakes
from their feathers. Late blooming branches droop beneath
sodden weight. From my kitchen window, I watch the squalls,
one on another, spill down from the distant mountains and
scale our meadow. I am a child again who cannot go out to
play.

No geese will ply today's skies, no birds extoll stippled

shelter. The woods bouquet on the table, gathered just yesterday, mocks my sullen senses. My trusty almanac describes May as "a songful promise, the idealization of spring." My almanac knows not this mountain's vagrant ways. It will take no less that a golden tomorrow to help me find forgiveness for this exalted season's broken vow.

But wait . . . is that the meadow lark's song rising? I run to the door, listen. Her liquid trill repeats from a snowy bower, proclaiming a faith less fickle than mine. The snows will melt then, the peas get planted. And for umbrella now, I'll use a snow-thatched greening tree.

One Hundred Sixty Acres
and Freedom

I've always suspected I was truant the day they taught measurements in school. Big ones, I mean. Rods, acres, miles. Anything up to a few feet I can handle, but the ruler in my cortex boggles at distance much beyond my own familiar shadow.

Brought up in Southern California, where if you were lucky your yard boasted two trees and a plot for petunias, I look over our farm's spread with a wild surmise. When the realtor first mentioned one hundred sixty acres, my vision balked, and I squelched an impulse to blurt, "Oh, we don't need *nearly* that many." But if any upstart today were to try to short me of one foot, one ponderosa's toehold or wild rose's shade, I'd feel my very soul threatened with thieving.

I still haven't absorbed it whole, all this space. Ten or twenty acres beyond my ken would have done nicely. And my heart's desire didn't demand this wealth of woods, the length of wild creek, the caverned draw over east where in spring a waterfall tumbles and benign snakes curl by the boulders to squint at the new sun. Being city refugees, we really didn't know what sort of spread would accommodate a vegetable garden big enough to feed us, a few goats and chickens, an occasional sacrificial pig or lamb. We knew even less how much *we'd* need to feel unfettered.

One hundred sixty acres, it turns out, suits us just fine. Five acres might give room for relative independence, but thirty-two times five guarantees freedom. Freedom for all the summer cocks to crow in unison before the hint of dawn and break no sleep but ours. Freedom for the goats to roam the woods, discover new wild greens to their liking, nibble at the barks of no one's trees. Freedom for the lady ducks to find a nesting place in some bushy bower, assured no neighbors' stock will trample the hatchery—provided the valley cows don't charge the hills and ford the creek and blunder through the barbed fences, which they blessedly rarely find initiative to do. Freedom for the dogs to run down the wind, to chase a promising scent or an alien sound to the farm's four corners, harrassing nary a soul but the rabbits and dreaming doves. Freedom for us human inhabitants to trudge the forest's maze for hours and find no human trash, no meddlesome improvement; to put Beethoven's Ninth on the record player and blast the dens and hollows with Judgment-Day sounds. (And the deer twitch their ears, and the rabbits dive for cover, and the jays fall strangely silent, their cocked crests flummoxed.)

If I hadn't been an avid ZPG'er before we moved to our mountain, I'd demand membership now. Creatures, human and of higher order, need *room*. Room with clean, green-nourished air to see through, crystal air, smelling of leaves and wind's cargo, air you can sniff with your eyes shut and define its season. A swathe of air up to the sky, and a sweep of sky to get giddy under, uncluttered for sunset and moonrise by any invention.

I don't know if the animals in our charge watch the sky cycles, note the moon shapes and star journeys. I do know that they raise a mighty chorus come dawn, crowing and bleating, pawing and baying to be let out to play, to celebrate the fact the sun indeed rose as on the first newfangled morning. And unlike Stevenson's child, in summer they wouldn't think to go to bed by day, unless dragged howling, nor in winter get up in seeming night. If the goats are milked and put to bed one speck before the fail of twilight, they grouch and snort hellfire, and anyone who has not tried to coax a wily chicken into the coop while the sun lingers knoweth not frustration. Nor can anyone deny that the coyote and wolf clans count, in some cortical corner, the nights toward the fattening moon. (Would a coyote warble in Manhattan, its view obstructed by the landlocked jungle—*if* it had breath left to howl with, given the city stench?)

I often tell our creatures how lucky they are with all this space, what crammed conditions some of their kin abide. The goats listen (goats are good listeners), then bound down the meadow, kicking up their heels to the rhythm of their clanging copper bells. The chickens gape, questioning my verity, and fly to the coop roof to spread the word. When I'm not holding them to lectures on their fortune, they often mob the woods in rooster-centered clutches, scratching the pine carpets to find a dust bath, pecking at pine nuts scrapped by the squirrels.

Minnie the pig was a master moat-digger, so she had to be confined behind an electrified fence. Her yard was large and lush with gourmet weeds, her chalet spacious and clean. Yet she spent the largest part of her hours gazing soulfully across the meadow to where the unfettered animals romped and roamed. Her yearning for release so weighted my conscience that I was as happy as she when she learned to short the wires and appeared at the doorstep on occasional mornings. I would join her then for a good chat and a walk along the woods'

fringes until it was time to accompany her back to *her* doorstep, with a sympathetic word about her lot and station. This
touch of freedom seemed to nourish her for days. Though I
was melancholy when she met her maker, I was glad for her
final emancipation. I hate to see a creature confined, hate to be
one.

Though we knew next to nothing about animal husbandry
when we started farming, our flocks and small herds have
seldom suffered a sick day. Our goats mother and milk to
perfection, their kids burst with well-being. The chickens are
kind and courteous to one another—but for the chauvinistic
cocks—and clean and capable about their henny habits. Even
the ducks are portraits of perfect duckdom. The rampant cats
and the dog family have never felt the breath of the diseases
that so often struck our city pets. We don't lay this circumstance to any special wisdom or scientific care, are in fact

still green to many farm ways. But we hold to a firm belief, born of our good experience and others' woes, that health and well being are nurtured by freedom and a wealth of space in which to celebrate it. It's hard to be sick or picky in the open air, in a stillness deep enough for a cricket to shatter, under a sky measured only by hawks' soar and wild geese wending.

Come winter snows, we tenderfoots swathe ourselves in scarves and boots and jackets and venture forth to tend the animals. The chickens hop one-footed atop the bundled earth; the goats plough through the drifts undaunted, their minds on play. The ducks parade the snowbound hill, skim splay-footed across their rimey pond. The dogs romp and run knee-deep, the deer criss-cross cloven paths all over the meadow. Chores done, we dash back to our fireside to rub our frozen fingers and stamp our feet to sensibility. The plummeting thermometer shrinks our boundaries, steely skies crowd us to the cabin's comforts. By February, our lungs feel full of woodsmoke, our heads of mold. The hardy creatures thrive, watch with pity and hauteur as we hug to our boards.

But even when the snows scud thickest and wintery winds howl down the hill bent on our eaves and chimneys, we peer out our windows or stop amid our chores to scan the weighted hills and measure our holdings. One hundred sixty acres. To play in, if we're brave; to web-foot about when cabin fever threatens, to hello over and listen for the frost-breathed reply. Sometimes the sound of a chain saw or plough rises from the Lapland of the valley. "Shh," we want to tell them, these disturbers of such peace. The sounds die away, snuffed finally by the hush of our hills.

Some day I mean to know each patch of our land by heart, to have touched the trunk of every tree. I've only memorized so far the hollow where the first March buttercup emerges, the deep woods den where the deer bed down, the brushy slope where the meadowlark returns each spring. Trees I hadn't noticed distract my explorations, log stumps in clearings invite simply sitting; a bird's ventriloquy can waylay me for hours.

The first time I ventured into our woods I got, before I had an inkling, lost. Leaning into a comforting boulder, I looked for familiars, the shadow of fear touching my shoulder. Silly, I told myself, how can you get lost on your own land? "Own" land, the woods mocked; who owns who now? Conceding they had a case, I sturdied my resolve and listened hard. A cockcrow drifted through the treetops, distant but with rescuing direction. Good friend, that bird. I'd have to remember to tell him. Gratefully, I tracked his raucous din out of the woods I knew now no one owned.

It is a loan, I've learned far better since, this land we claim. A place to cohabit with those who do know it by heart, and by an instinct better honed than mine.

No, we don't really need one hundred sixty acres, don't utilize but a small portion. But that's the beanty of such spacious holdings: we know it's there, untrammeled, sanctified. We can return its gift of freedom by letting it *be*.

APOSTROPHE II

Shooting Stars

"Ooh, did you see that one?" In the starlight, his eyes are like saucers. "Did you? Its tail went for miles!"

"No, darn, I missed it, where?"

"Up there, you should have *seen* it." He points to a place in the sky where the stardust is thickest. I look for a sign.

One should always watch shooting stars with a child. Their eyes have bigger corners, their wonder's contagious.

"That's, let's see, forty-six now for me. How many do you have?"

"Um, only forty," I confess. "You're a better star-watcher than me." (You don't have to remember proper English with children, with stars.)

It is true. He notices things; things like lizards sunning themselves on old boards, and toads' eyes watching from hollows. He isn't distracted by this or that to be done, by Direction.

"Look, look there. See those eyes?" Holding his breath, he points to twin gleams in the dark. "What do you s'pose they are?"

"One of the cats, I'd guess. See, they're moving now. Probably a cat coming home from a mouse-hunt."

"No, I think it's a beast of some sort, maybe a werewolf, or a tiger. Boy, we'd better stay very still. It might climb up on this porch here and *eat* us."

I obey, daring not even a whisper. He's right, it could be a tiger, in a child's apparition of night. In the shared, scared silence, I drift back to a time when each shadow in every dark corner had fangs, and that tap of a branch on the pane was a claw scratching and the beast's belly growled from the bushes. Fun to be scared now, to feel the skin crawl, with reason at hand when the shapes get too real for indulgence. Nice not to have to give reason for everything.

"Ooh, look, another one. Didn't you see?"

Lord, I missed that one too. Why am I always looking somewhere else when they fall? (Well, someone has to watch out for tigers.)

"That was a super-duper. I wish Mark were here to see."

Mark is his brother. I'm glad he's not with us tonight. He is older than David, two or three years, too old now to amaze at just stars. He knows reasons, can tell you the name of each constellation, and even what men found on the moon and how they arrived. Especially how they arrived. He'll probably grow up to be a scientist. He's fond of becauses and hows.

Star light, star bright, fortieth star I see tonight . . .

"Aw, I'm up to forty-nine," David says. "The fiftieth should be something special. I should have wished on every one of them. Just think, fifty wishes."

"Could you make up that many?"

He grins. "I guess not. I know, I could wish for fifty *more.* Let's stay here all night, okay?"

David might grow up to be a poet. He doesn't care any more than I try not to for becauses and hows.

There's not the smallest orb
which thou behold'st
But in his motion
like an angel sings . . .

Yes, a poet. One should always watch shooting stars with a growing-up poet.

A fleck bursts across the east edge of the sky, its tail flicking dragontooth embers. "Ooh," we both gasp, then look at each other, amazed.

"That was a giant," says David. "I think it landed somewhere, over in those mountains, see?"

I nod. "It must have," I agree. "Maybe it sank from its weight all the way to the earth's core."

"At least all the way to the ocean, I bet. Maybe somebody'll find it floating on the waves. Do you suppose?"

The little stars were the herring fish
That lived in the beautiful sea . . .

"I hope so. I hope it lights some sailor's way."

We pull the blanket over our knees and stare up again at the sky shapes. There is no sound but our gentle breathing. One must be very still to catch falling stars. One must watch with a child who senses such secrets.

Maybe tomorrow I'll go looking for lizards, pass some time with a toad. One shouldn't put off such chances on a steady, singular star.

Weathering

To "weather," my good Webster's explains, is, among other things, "to wear away, discolor, disintegrate," or "to pass through safely, survive." Inhabitant now of a north country mountain, I couldn't put it better. Maybe it was all those years of a tropical clime that left me unprepared, or maybe it's my sky signs. All I know is that my body and mind expand and contract with the seasons, are at the mercy of every wind shift, arctic blast and sun blessing that march up our mountain from directions only a mad genie could establish.

This is not a lament, mind you, but objective observation. It isn't as though some force plucked me from my sunny shore and bound me to this Promethean rise. I chose it, with the weather gods my witness.

You see, I *wanted* weather, hungered for nuances beyond sea fog and balmy brightness. Forty-odd snowless Christmases, and Easters scarcely distinguishable from Hallowe'ens, left me with a gaping curiosity about my earth ship's vicissitudes, about the feel of its tilt and yaw. So when we were snowed in from our first winter solstice until mid-January, I thought it the height of adventure, and when summer lightning storms played havoc in our dens and copses, I felt at last in touch with the elements, awesome though they might be. When the winter thermometer plunged to $-20°$ and the Ashley began hyperventilating, I fantasized myself as Admiral Peary, Sherpa Tensing, the Ice Queen all in one heroic form. Brave, sturdy, just a soupçon superior I was to all those naifs left behind, those sun cultists with nothing better to do than compare suntan oils and degrees of melanin.

But when the chickens' claws froze to their feed trays and the clothes froze like steam-rollered demons to the line and the power lines toppled from their cargo of ice and the goat droppings froze in clumps all over the milking stand, I was sore pressed to pause and reconsider. They had looked so pretty, all those winter pictures, the Curriers and Ives seemed so clean and jolly. But then comes a day when the sun bursts over the hill and the ice droplets on every branch become diamonds and eaves-icicles prisms, and the snow is just right for snowmen and snowballs and snow angels, and the ice caves on the creek are crystal domes and one can't get enough to store of every metamorphosed nook and cranny.

We had thought when we moved here that we'd stocked up pretty well with winter vesture. Mike, dredging memories of New England's ice-bound seasons, became the expert outfitter. Wool jackets, brushed flannel shirts, thermal long johns, a raft of heavyweight socks, vibrum-soled ankle boots, unprocessed wool helmets, those were the ticket. And we spent half the first winter piling the garments on for venturings out or pulling them off for indoor doings, and the first time I dared the snow-laden meadow I was so immobilized by my bundledness that I fell promptly into a drift and had to be rescued, spitting and flailing, by an errant knight in only slightly less weighty armor. Layering is fine in concept, if one doesn't carry it so far as to lose one's motility. And though long johns are salvation for long stays out-of-doors,

I found them itchily confining within speaking distance of the wood stove.

Years of applied analysis have since taught me that if my head, extremities and chest are warm, the rest of the moving body (and who sits still in sub-freezing degrees?) bears up well. So, though wool sweaters, scarves, mittens, jackets, hats and sheepskin-lined boots sit ready at the cabin door, the only bow I make to Siberian weathers in the rest of my wardrobe is to wear heavier jeans. And on those rare nights when a blizzard roars up the mountain, and two Ashleys roaring twin hellfires can't hold the blasting cold at bay, I don the voluminous skirt I patched up one winter out of old blankets, tuck my triple-socked feet underneath and listen cozily to the chimney's rattle and the old boards' groan. Mike sits nearby in his venerable Indian blanket robe, a great, frayed tent of a vestment we found one year at the Heppner Rummage. ("Silas wore that 'til the day he died," a china teacup of a lady whispered to us, smoothing the patched elbow. Bless Silas, his passage was toasty.)

One concession we wouldn't be caught dead of frostbite making is the purchase of an electric blanket, an item we consider a decadent misuse of energy. Conservation aside, the thing wouldn't do us much good anyhow, since it's usually on the weatheriest of nights that the power fails . . . an event brought on, we suspect, from everyone else turning up their wired contraptions to nine. There is seldom need for such extravagance, for the heat radiating from the pipe which rises through the loft from the stove below keeps the vaulted room amazingly comfortable, despite its unadorned four view windows. On those nights when my blanket skirt and old Silas's robe are called for, we simply pile pillows against the panes, add Grandmother's quilt to the bedcovers, and, since human bodies are the best bedwarmers, snuggle the polar night away.

Still a sun idolator, I sometimes nurse a winter wonder of how I ended up so blasted far from the equator. Then, come the first pastel days of spring, with their advent of prodigal birds and jubilation of wild flowers, days when the chickens scratch at the emerged earth and prattle joyously, and the goats think they're leggy kids again and gambol up and down the steps, and the dogs laze in the sun gnawing recovered bones, and the ducks splash orgiastically in the snowmelt puddles, I remember, I know. No humdrum clime could hold a candle to a radiant spring day on our mountain meadow, no tropic ease compete with these blooming seasons.

We count our seasons not so much by the calendar, an implement too arbitrary for this high desert, mountain-capped inland, as by our cabin and farm-borne activities. Three balmy April days in a row, and the winter clothes get packed away, the cut-off jeans and tennies pulled out, aired and re-shaped by the breezes. (This is a guaranteed way to bring on the next snowstorm, but one must acknowledge the earth-shaking event, must display one's gratitude.) A full week without the need of woodstove fires, and I clear and sweep the log bin corner, scrub all the windows of their winter smoke. (There will be further fires, into June, most likely, but ah, the chair looks nice back in that corner, and the panes so pristine.) Ten days of frostless nights and I'm in a panic to get the seeds into their greenhouse flats, to air out the root cellar, to clear my dooryard garden of its winter wrack. (There will be frosts again, 'til who knows when, but the plumb of my spirit yearns to tend green.)

Then May, and the apples blossom, and a walk down the hillside is a tour of a perfumery, and the pink-tongued white clouds swallow up the greening slope of meadow. And just when the blossoms are fully unfurled and the sallow flesh shows signs of healthy color and the wild violets lift their petals to the growing brightness, it ups and snows. And I wonder what a sun idolator is doing so blasted far from the equator. But as the soft spring blanket insulates the bloom-ing growth from harm, it also insulates the psyche. "This is probably the last snow until winter," we tell each other; and each flake, like the apple petals, becomes precious in its de-clining. "Winter lingering chills the lap of May . . . ," but we have made safe passage. Worn away, discolored, disin-tegrated, we are rescued by spring.

APOSTROPHE III

Summer's End

Mid-autumn only, with winter's breath on the air, and
nothing goes right with the farm chores. Not yet into that
time of daylight's brief visits when the woodpile is sure salvation and the hours are compassed by stove's and body's
feeding, the comforts of roof, food and warmth, neither are
we ready yet to let go our hold of this season. There are leaves
yet hugging the trees, the meadow and dooryard still show
patches of fading green.

It is somehow a comfort to note that the animals are as
testy as we. The chickens strut stiff-legged and glare at their
diminished shadows. The goats short their giving. The ducks
huddle around those places where warm, grubby earth used
to be. Cats circle the stove, waiting, remembering how the
hearth felt when their windowsills froze, when the grasses
they used to hide in were no longer tall and green.

"They're drinking all the milk I need for cheese," Mike
complains, watching the cats' bowl empty.

"No more than always," I say. "It's just that the goats are
holding back, and that darn kid won't wean."

"Hey, how come I only get one egg for breakfast?"

"The hens miss their sunshine, or maybe the dogs know
nests I haven't found."

"Some of those hens are senile. We really should slaughter."

"I think they're just molting," I tell him. "Let's wait and
see."

It's so hard now to remember the more generous seasons, so easy to think this winter's harbingers bode the leanest ever. Surely the chickens produced longer before, surely the goats were more generous as breeding season neared. Surely the mornings weren't this cold, the stove in need of stoking so often through the day.

One evening in chill October, we have our first of the season's flue fires. Nothing serious, these small flare-ups happen every year. We watch the stovepipe for a telltale glow, watch the chimney pot to see that embers don't settle where they'll feed. The room grows stifling; the floor stays icy. We argue over whether we should open the door for fresh air or just let the fire die. Before that is settled, the radio station giving us Vivaldi sputters and fades. "I *know* we used to get that station better in winter," Mike moans. But it is not yet winter. This is that chill no-man's-land between.

Winters, you expect things, know the rituals. Know the bundling up and hand-rubbing charges outdoors, know keeping an ear tuned through the night to the logs' crackling, lest waking limbs freeze. Know to keep the tap trickling so the water won't ice, and heating pailsful for the creatures at all hours. You accept eggs being sparse and goats grouchy; you sympathize. It's the betweenness that startles, the reluctance to let go of the sun's glitter, to give up carpets of green. It's too soon for tree limbs naked, too soon to be dark by five. And, good lord, look where the Pleiades have moved to already!

Yet, take heart, we tell each other; this too will pass, we say. Winter doth make way for spring, and once Christmas is past, the seed catalogues will start arriving, and frozen limbs will feel their urgent stirring. And before that, there'll be the snowbirds to study, snowflakes to mark, tracks to trace across the powdered meadow. (But, oh, I had thought *this* summertime would stay, and then, that gold and crimson would wash the hillside longer; thought this time I was better rehearsed.)

Let's have it then, since nothing will stay it, "the rawish dank of clumsy winter" with its "wan, bleak cheek." If earth knew naught but summer, how would her charges value rank green and gold? Stoke up the fire, line boots beside the door. Pin a seed packet to the cupboard as a memento; pin a hope to the battened door.

(But, oh, I had thought that summer . . . and then the crimson, gold would this time stay. . . .)

Cabin Fever:

No Known Fatalities

February is the worst, the local wags say, the month when winter often spills her pent-up vengeance. While the thermometer stays stuck at zero, we reach into the pit of our endurance and come up scant. The forest road is packed with foot-high snow, and hiking out on the riven lower road is a possibility only dire circumstance could urge, for our faces stiffen with cold in just the time it takes to perform minimal chores. The outhouse is an icebox, and the animals' water turns solid before we finish their housekeeping.

The stove crackles and puffs hour on hour, its belly forcefed at each new draft, and nighttimes we have to fill the door cracks with sweaters where the cats tore off the weather stripping. Pillows are piled for the duration against the upstairs windows, shutting out the ghostly light. Hawk-eyed, we watch each other to see that neither, in an absent funk, turns off the tap's full trickle again.

Tylwyth has all but closed up her milk factory, and the chickens give but three or four pale yolks a day. The outside cats huddle in the windowsills, little match girls envying the square of warmth beyond the panes. The dogs shiver at the door, assuming expressions of soulful courage each time we, bulwarked and balaclava'd, forge outside. The woodpile, which looked so mountainous at winter's entry, would now cast but a thin shadow, if there were shadow to cast in this somber, crabbed land.

Evenings, I ruffle through seed catalogues as devotedly as I would utter prayers. Their bright colors and promise of lush vegetables and posies are another planet, a place where winter traipses gracefully, where calendars skip right past January into March. I sweep the cabin, bake the bread, mend, sew. Mike types and reads halfheartedly, and worries, over tedious columns, about this year's finances. The early stars grow distant, fleeing the cold.

The fat of long-lost Christmas sits upon us, slowing our

sluggish ways. Before morning energies arise, it's afternoon, and before afternoon's chores are done, it's evening. Under a pile of quilts, we read late into the nights, our cold hands stiff around the saving pages, our fingers numbing. The mind, we vow, won't atrophy, though the world's a world away.

I get a headache, Mike's back hurts. I'm tempted to kick a cat, Mike curses the sick typewriter. Psychosoma pervades and testiness burgeons.

"If we could just get to the postbox!"

"I wonder what the Sunday paper says, and the Sunday's before that."

"Would you *please* fix the goatbarn gate for me? I'm tired of kicking it open against the snow."

"You turned off the light in the root cellar and the damn sauerkraut froze!"

"This dumb kindling is frozen to the woodbox."

Bitch, bitch, bitch, and groan about an ache here, a stiffness there, and heft our sun-starved bodies to the chores that, once fun, seem torpid burdens. And peer out doors and windows, aching for a sign of spring, for mending summer, golden autumn, for any season but this ice-locked hinterland. We are a century old, we should be bears and simply hibernate until the world turns round, should be bugs wombed in warm cocoons. Spring is too far behind for bearing.

Yet beyond winter's bearing, we hold a trust by now that even this won't last forever, that three blood-quickening seasons spoil us. We remember, however dimly, that when the icicles melt from the eaves, the garden plans will come to life, that when the earth finally emerges, the first robin will be there to share the celebration. And we know best of all that this winter weight, this snow, cold, ice-bound space is better by far than city streets and earth-divested comforts.

You don't get cabin fever in the city; neither do you find

thereabout the specific of the first woods buttercup promising a transmuted season, a round of celebrations only country dwellers are invited to share.

APOSTROPHE IV

A Promise of Spring

Earth feels its solstice. Small green sprouts push up from the forest floor, delicate ferns and maroon seedlings, green leaves no bigger than raindrops, and the other day, the surprise of one new wild strawberry leaf. Though I know it's too soon yet, my annual watch for spring's first buttercup begins.

Just last night, a drip-drip from the eaves remarked the silence, and by midnight soft snow iced the ground. But the jays this morning woke us, announcing a morning brilliance of newborn sun.

The deer families have been nonchalant about their visits this winter, haven't needed our meadow's provision; there are enough feeding spaces unburied in the higher woods. Still, they gather at the pines' edge every evening as though keeping an eye on our season's progress. At their first footfall, the dogs dance and bark up a commotion. We let them think they hold the deer at bay. God knows, they need some sense of accomplishment, a reason for being beyond harrassing chickens.

There is a bird who comes daily now to the highest pear tree branch. He perches there and emits over and over one piercing tenor note. Though we suspect he's a Townsend's

Solitaire, we call him our radar bird and carry on guessing games about what it is he signals. Secretly, I think it is spring, but to say so aloud might tempt a last wintery blast of retribution.

There are other signs. Last week a cloud of robins filled the orchard in what appeared a celebration of some sort, perhaps of the nodules fuzzing on the apple branches. We even debate some mornings whether to fire up the wood stove, and though we usually, teeth chattering, give in, there are days when the door is flung wide by midmorning, when the cats leave their huddle by the fire and curl into patches of sunlight laid across the floor.

My garden seeds and sets are sorted and piled in a ready basket. I count them over, dreaming of warm earth, of May. "Hurry," I plead with the fickle sun, "give me a sign that my faith be renewed." And the next day, there on the creek bank alongside the woods road, willow catkins burst into feather, defying the slate-colored sky. It is promise enough.

Celebrations
and Ceremonies...

Spring is a maverick season in this corner of the country, arriving in fits and starts sometimes in March, sometimes not until late May. May? I can't remember an early June I didn't take my pea packets to the garden, full of greening intent, only to get blue-fingered by a sudden frigid gust or blinded by snow flurries. Yet in the face of such inconstant weather, come Easter, and I pull out all the stops to celebrate earth's renaissance. Perfect days need no ceremony; it is the dour and disappointing which beg festivity.

One blustery Easter, I built on a hillside promontory a miniature Stonehenge of flat rocks. The cats, thinking it a lovely playground, soon had it in shambles, but not before I peered at the pale sun through its chinks and made up a mock druid prayer. For another Easter, I dyed a batch of eggs and hid them in clumps around the meadow. That they were gone by the next day proved someone was enriched by tradition. The dogs looked awfully pleased. Then there was the Easter Sunday we feasted on a huge, rosy ham, the final gift of Buster the pig. Nostalgia hung like a cloud over the table. "Remember the time he escaped and led the others into the woods, then marched them back in parade at sunset?" I asked.

"And I yelled 'sooey sooey' until I was hoarse. . . ." Mike chuckled.

"And how he used to tip over his water trough the minute I filled it, then look up and grin—"

"And the way he crawled under the hay with just his snout showing, surveying his realm. . . ."

"Bless Buster, I hope he understands."

"Now, don't go getting upset, we raised him for the likes of this ham."

"No, no . . . it's just—"

But after dinner, I take the leftover squash to Minnie so she too can celebrate. She downs the serving in one gulp, then comes to the fence for a head scratch. "We entreat for them Thy mercy and Thy pity," I recite, but the prayer doesn't seem joyous for Easter, so I make up another. "Let me believe the flesh I eat is reborn in me." Minnie grunts, and I feel better.

One Easter, wanting a proper commemoration, we raked and piled the damp garden refuse and lit a bonfire, to tempt the sun's return to our farm quarter. It spat and smouldered and died in a disheartening heap, and the next day the snow returned to hang bleakly about for a week. Such impoverished pagans, we, dumb as to what deities to call on for winter's surcease.

Hallowe'en carries a more solid guarantee. If the autumn is fitting, the occasion falls among those days of fiery sunsets and twilights the color of deep mountain dens, when gold and rust pear and apple leaves lick the hillside's fading green. In the quick snuff of darkness, we light the carved pumpkin's candle, watch the wicked eyes fire, the snaggletoothed grin gleam, then carry it to the porch table for the warding off of hallowed spites. Though no human beggars trudge up the dark and distant mountain to our door, for old times' sake, and mine, I keep sweets at hand: platters of fudge and jars of raisin-eyed cookies, shortbreads drizzled with shrewish orange-ice faces. And through the bewitched night, while Mike sips his brew and reads, as though the slipping hours were quite empty of portent, I hold the haunts at bay by nibbling my way through the sweets until by the stroke of midnight, the pit of my spirit is bolstered and my body too heavy to fly. If the moon chances to rise by bedtime, I watch it from my window, scanning its face for the shadow of a flapping shape. The goblins'll getcha if you don't watch out, taunt indigestible dreams.

Then Thanksgiving, heavy with winter's traces. By now, fall's tawny colors are gone, the hills are subdued and monotonous. Jays arrive in droves to lord the trees, the last independent banty rooster forsakes his night watch from the pear tree and returns to the fold. For days before the holiday, we survey the cocks, trying to recall who was hatched when and which tend to skirmish with their weaker kin.

"Look at *his* spurs," says Mike. "He has to be on his last legs!"

"That happens to be Peter the III and, though long in tooth, he's a perfect gentleman."

"Okay, but that multicolored one has been around for a while."

"Motley? But he's gorgeous, the most handsome of all. Just look at those feathers."

"What about the white one there, who's he?"

"Sam? That's the one Si gave us because of his good lineage. We can't kill *him*."

"Maybe we should just splurge and buy a turkey," Mike sighs. Which we do, rationalizing what cheap meals the bird will provide, never mind his unnatural upbringing. And Motley and Peter the III and all their kin are off the hook again, to wax into their dotage, to keep the fiesty youngsters in line. I ask you, did the Pilgrims stoop to base chicken, even in *their* penury?

We counted five wild turkeys on our land of a recent season, big, placid birds, looking much smarter than they're credited to be. Some time later, a valley farmer confessed he'd brought them here because he wanted them to produce and flourish, and knew we'd let them be. Sure enough, in summer's wane, we spied two hens conducting a clutch of youngsters through the brush, dangerously close to the creek crossing where deer hunters set up autumn camp. But there was no way we could coax the wildlings to a safer shade. "We entreat for them Thy mercy and Thy pity" was again a futile prayer. Deer-hunting season was worse than usual that year, with overeager sportsmen vying for each foot of the creekside space. We've not seen nor heard a sign of the birds since. Friends brought a market turkey to us that Thanksgiving, but the meal, for me, lacked festivity. I'd gladly have traded a dozen of his kind for that crescendoed gobble, the pleasure of our lost birds' courtly company.

I think it must be during the Christmas season that north country living reaches perfection. Oh, there are June days aplenty one would like to make last forever, but summer's youth is flawless worldwide. Though I may grow restive in January, August, November, yearn for a flash of city lights, the feel of close friends near, I can't imagine spending a Christmas time beyond our snowbound meadow, our chimney'd cabin, our fresh-cut, perfect Christmas tree. (Each, in fickle memory, more perfect in shape, scent and size than the one before.) Our Christmas ceremonies are quiet, and in that quietude we find rare peace. We're sometimes forlorn, for few

friends or family hazard wintery back-country travel, but in
that aloneness is space to sense the event's history. Our gifts
are few, shops being out of reach and our budget narrow,
but the look of the sharp-shadowed meadow endows us, and
the cabin windows aglow, the yule log's soliloquy. The first
Christmas was simple and animal-befriended; so, at Christmas, are we.

Yet the holy day here doesn't want for celebration, despite
our isolation and semi-poverty. Once the tree is decked and
the cards strung on the windowsills (if we can't reach the
postbox, I string up last year's) and the old Christmas books
of childhood piled on the tables and the creche set in its bower
and the records full of glory music stacked on the turntable,
the oven goes into full-time production. Cookies, tarts, pies,
breads are popped into and offered from it day upon day.
Have to have sweets ready, for Joe and Phillippa are coming, if the roads are open, and maybe this year Luce and
Elsie will brave the snows, and Penny might be able to fly into
Portland, then take a bus to Redmond, then hitch a ride—if
the weather is kind. And the Randalls might come down the
mountain, if they're not snowed in (little Charlie loves my
cookies), and the Palmers might come up, if they can get
through the slough, and maybe Amy will drop by on her
cross country skiing trek.

Just maybe; but it doesn't matter. Christmas is lovely to
share, Christmas is wondrous to spend in solitude. If no one
can reach our weathered mountain, we'll split the sweetmeats
with the creatures (Sable loves my madeleines), and warble
our carols into their indulgent ears. Guests or not, each
Christmas Eve, donning scarves and caps and mittens, we
crunch down the crisping hillside to the goat barn, the coop,
Noel-ing, Tannenbaum-ing quietly so as not to startle the
goats, the chickens, the staring stars. They listen, all three.

The chimney smoke drifts over the meadow, the pine boughs glitter at the meadow's edge; the cabin's panes cast golden patchwork onto the snow.

"Look, Mike, look at that biggest star."

"Mm-hmm, that's the one."

"Let's wish on it, a joyous Christmas."

On our simple mountain, it is indeed.

It's not just the official holidays that call for special observance. The farm makes its own occasions for festivity, small achievements and entries that invite private celebration, which is sometimes the best kind of all. The placing of the last log on the five-cord woodpile demands a toast to winter comfort and a few hours off for play. Maybe we'll pack a picnic, go up to the place on the creek where Indians once camped and scrounge for arrowheads under the trees, or drive up to the summit and look through the woods for this year's Christmas tree. Whatever the recreation, we'll be sure, before dark, to survey the towering woodpile and know the meaning of security.

And then there's June's first ripe strawberry, found sitting jewel-like in a nest of leaves. Finding it, I look around furtively, making sure no one might claim it, then pop it into my mouth and shut my eyes, that no other sense distract the taste of its sun-warm juice trickling down my gullet. When there are handfuls, I will share, when bucketsful, make jams and jellies. None will taste as sweet or look as plumply rosy as this summer harbinger.

The first red tomato, on the other hand, has flesh enough for sharing. I carry it up from the garden as though it were a king's ransom, find Mike in his workshop and offer him the first bite.

"Radio warns of pockets of frost tonight," he says, wiping his chin. Oh mortal messenger, unworthy of summer's blessings. But fortune shines, that year or another, and the tomatoes burgeon. Most are eaten the day they are picked, when they are still firm and sweet. Elsie's recipe makes of them our favorite appetizer:

Slice tomatoes into bowl, add dash of olive oil and salt, snip in equal pieces of fresh basil and mint to taste. Let sit awhile for flavors to meld.

It is my firm opinion that the Garden of Eden must have boasted tomatoes and basil, hand in hand. My only wonder is how the first earthly family could truly enjoy the combination without a cold glass of goat buttermilk on the side. Or did the Good Book include goats in Paradise? If not, it was a glaring oversight, and not at all like Him.

Yet even the garden's loot pales beside the first breath of flesh and blood creatures. I'd be surprised if the heart of the gruffest curmudgeon wouldn't leap to hear a muffled cheeping under a mother hen's fluff, or to watch an egg crack and a curious eye gape through the breach at its brave new world.

No matter how faithfully I mark my calendar, no matter how prodigiously keep my farm notes, births and hatchings are always amazements. This is due, I suppose, to my skepticism that live beings can take shape and be born within such a short span; that from a speckled yolk, the very sort we take at daily breakfast, a lively, inquisitive chick can be formed in much less time than a bean takes in growing or an apple to form from its bud. Surely if one wants for miracles, he can look to the earth's egg producers.

"Mike, guess what? Pinky hatched three chicks since yesterday!"

"I didn't even know she was brooding."

"Neither did I. She's been hiding under the goats' manger."

"Don't you think we should move her into the pen?"

"No-o, not yet, she's still got a big clutch under her."

And the next day, five chicks bob about the goat barn, pecking at each seed their mother includes in their lessons, and a few days on there are eleven. We catch them one by one, tuck protesting Pinky under an arm, and transfer the lot to the pen. By dark, they are back under the manger, the brood tucked beneath Pinky's down. So for a week we expand the farm ritual to include toting the family to their proper quarters, and for a week, find them each morning back in their nursery.

"We can't leave them there," Mike protests, "the goats

will stomp them." But the goats gape at their tiny roommates
and walk around them most carefully. If Tylwyth, Sable and
Blossom don't mind the intrusion, why should I?

Six months later, I mind, but by then the settlement is way
beyond our foreclosure. Eleven young hens traipse faithfully
at sunset into the goat barn, accompanied by two roosters
with evil intent and a waylaid old granny. In the dusk, when
we enter to milk, they're roosting cozily, on the stanchion,
the manger, the patient goats' spines. By morning the once
pristine barn is a mess. "Shoo!" I flail at them with my broom.
"Bug off!" Mike hollers. One lands on my shoulder, clucking softly, another pecks at Mike's shoelace. A peaceable
kingdom, untidy but comradely as all get out. Mike threatens, come spring, to slaughter them all. I suggest we might
just build a new goat barn, a great length from the coop,
and let the chicks fall where they may.

By seasons and miles, the worthiest cause for celebration
is the arrival of goat kids. I had, in my pre-country days, witnessed only the entries of pups, kittens and human babes.
Each filled me with awe and a sense of my own wondrous
being. Yet never could I have imagined a newborn, still wet
from the sac, prancing, remarking, inviting the midwife, the
mother, the milking stool even to play. I can't dream why
some worthy scientist doesn't study the contents of the goat
cortex and DNA to discover what element flourishes there to
create such newborn brightness, such rampant vitality. If it
could be isolated, the ingredient might well improve sober
mankind.

Until that unlikely time, we greet the goat kids with delight, knowing they will hazard and rupture and brighten
our days beyond measure. We can't keep them forever, of
course; we haven't the time, room nor need for an expanded

goat family. But tell me, please, what more precious under heaven remains?

There are those who claim miracles no longer happen, are passé. Gardeners, husbandmen, earth kinsmen know better. We are privileged to watch and share rebirth and creation, the hungry reach of each plant and being for its place in the sun. Celebrating the marvels of nature's turns and inventions reminds us of our own awesome genesis and the place we are given to share it. That's miracle enough for me.

APOSTROPHE V

Christmas on the Mountain

Some quiet hour of each Yuletide season, I call back the ghosts of Christmases past: all those city holidays celebrated during all those city-yoked years. Neither more nor less happy or festive or all the things Christmas should be, they were . . . well, as different from country Christmases as morning from night.

For one thing, there were the last-minute shopping forays (the season tending to sneak in unexpectedly amid balmy days and flowers still in bloom) past glittering shop windows and into jampacked store aisles, followed by bumbling attempts to fit oneself and armsful of assorted packages into bus or taxi (when the latter could be hailed, which was seasonally rare) for a traffic-embattled trip home.

And then there was the tree selection, the pokings into

midtown lots thronged with orphaned pines and firs, to survey which offered the bushiest, the freshest, the grandest assortment, or, if that choice was too hard, which tree lot at-
tendant looked most forlorn or needy. If the kids were along,
the selection could consume a whole evening. Penny always
wanted the tallest, one whose crowning star would touch the
ceiling; Steve's preference was for symmetry ("Not *that* one,
look at the gap in its branches, ugh!"), while Brad invariably
found the saddest, scrawniest, most unkempt of all, because
"No one even looks at it, Mom, the poor, sad thing." Sometimes we ended up buying all three because each claim was
so convincing and, well, it was just once a year. Furniture
would have to be shoved aside and extra lights unearthed
and enough silver tinsel icicles bought to hide the imperfec-
tions that never showed until the tree was tugged and tilted
and stuck in its home corner. One year, we journeyed to a
tree farm far from home to buy a living tree, considering it a
special treat to dig it up ourselves and heft its incensed freshness into our unaccommodating car. Once the holiday was
spent, we planted Tree in an honored garden spot, envisioning the shade and scent it would offer as it flourished. But
alas, the tired, weighted, culture-shocked thing died before
it even saw spring. Since we hadn't the heart to toss it away,
it probably still stands in that old garden, a barren monu-
ment to the city dweller's folly.

And then there were the ritual holiday parties with their
clamor of hearty talk over clinking glasses, the strained attempts at rare camaraderie. No one felt, in his heart, that they
had much to do with the true Christmas spirit, but hadn't
we always had them? And, well, it was just once a year.

Christmas Eve then, with carols around the lighted, laden
tree, the children eyeing their packages knowingly and beg-
ging to stay up just a few minutes longer, for just one more

carol, or maybe we could open just one gift each, oh please? And always, I remember, when all was still and everyone tucked into Christmas dreams, I would sit in the darkened room beside a window and try to find in the sky a star that looked somehow special, a star brighter alone than all the massed indoor ornament; a star that spoke of hope and renewal and my childhood fantasies.

And now, on this mountain, I look out the cabin window, out past the tree shadows on the meadow, the familiar farm shapes. All is still. The carols have been sung to the hushed hilltop, toasts offered, candles lit to warm the old walls' apparitions. The star I used to wish on glitters beyond the frost-fingered panes. But my old wish is granted. I have my country Christmas, my simple creatures, my woods to walk in, and the peace to explore this fulfillment.

All the glittering ghosts of Christmases past could never match the mountain's holy silence, or its kinship to that ancient Christmas Eve.

...And Infelicities

It's New Year's Eve, and just when we're ready to hoist a toddy, the cabin is plunged into darkness. By now I know by heart the paths to the candles and oil lamps, and within minutes, their flickerings pool kitchen and parlor table, dance on the walls. Nice, for New Year's Eve. And somehow, as it does each time the power dies, a deep stillness settles, as though darkness muffles all sound. This is soon broken by the battery radio's hiss, Mike trying to tune in the Co-op crew to find out where and when. A voice breaks through, "It's out of our hands, fellows. Bonneville's out. Ice on the lines all the way to the Columbia." Grim news; we might be without power for quite a spell.

But by morning, we have lights again, and the indulgence of the electric stove. Well, then, I'll bake bread, make a yeasty entry into the new year. Mid-afternoon, just as I slide the loaves into the oven, poof, the oven light dims and goes dark. Blast! By the time I get the Majestic fired up properly, the loaves will have fallen. I wrap them and dash them to the freezer. Good luck, you white monster, and may your heart remain stone-cold.

Two weeks later, Superbowl Sunday. During breakfast, the power again fails. "Uh-oh," Mike groans, "not *today*!" Within two hours, the power is back, but the TV antenna system isn't. "They'll fix it," he assures himself. "Everyone in town will be waiting for the game." But they don't. The hour arrives, passes.

Mike glares at the empty screen, fiddles with the radio, calls a neighbor. "Ray's out of town," she explains. "I guess it won't get fixed 'til he gets back." Mike pictures Ray, the fixer, in some alien corner of civilization, watching each play in living color. He goes outside to chop some wood, a good outlet for high dudgeon.

We pay fifteen dollars a year to help maintain the TV translator which sits atop the hairbreadth scarp of yonder hill. For this, we get three commercial channels. Sometimes. Seldom when there's a prize play scheduled, or a major news event breaks.

"Hooray, *The Godfather*'s going to be on NBC. We'll finally get to see it!"

"Want to bet?" asks Mike. No thank you, I know the odds.

I once remarked to a townie how awful the reception had been of late. "It's always like that in the summer," she said. And to another that we'd missed Cronkite for two weeks because CBS was missing. "It always gets bad in the winter," she said.

We turn, for diversion, to the radio. One or two nights a week during winter we can get classics from a station two states away, or news commentary from Canada—until, that is, the notes fade and the voices garble. One day I will write a program of my own, one which asks the question, "Can a media freak, a news monger find happiness in a land of electronic ineptitude?" Tune in tomorrow, a small voice says; silence is golden, it taunts. The heck, I answer, feeding on fantasies of televised PBS treasures.

Then March, and I make an article deadline just under the wire. I ask Mike if he wants to hike to the car and drive to the postbox with me. (My motive is ulterior; I'm all thumbs with tire chains.) "No way," says he. "The road is a quagmire."

"We could chain up."

"We already are, and we're still stuck."

"But my deadline. . . ."

"I know," he consoles. "Maybe tomorrow, if we get a heavy freeze." Glaring down the oozing hillside, I consider another profession; a professional hermit, perhaps, or a raiser of carrier pigeons.

One morning, I bite down on a mean, unsprouted mungbean, and a tooth crumbles onto my tongue. Ow! I rush to the phone, and, lisping, call the dentist. It is Friday, and he is fifty miles away. He'll see me Monday, he says, but Sunday night, eight inches of snow skulk over the mountain. I call again. I'll be late. Will he wait for me?

"Better not try today," he warns, "The roads are black ice all the way." Toothless in Gaza, I despair. Gaza would be easier, it never snows there.

Mike gets, one wintery night, what threatens to be terminal food poisoning. Scared to death, I try to call the doctor, but the phones are on the fritz again. I pull him through with promises to all my saints and doses of chamomile tea. Once the crisis is past, the phone is magically mended, and we return to the minor frustration of squeezing an occasional smatter of words through the neighborly four-party line.

"Oh, sorry to interrupt, Alice, but this is Joan, and I need to report a fire."

"Oh, hi. A fire, huh? Where's it at?"

"The smoke's coming from beyond the west knoll. It's pretty heavy."

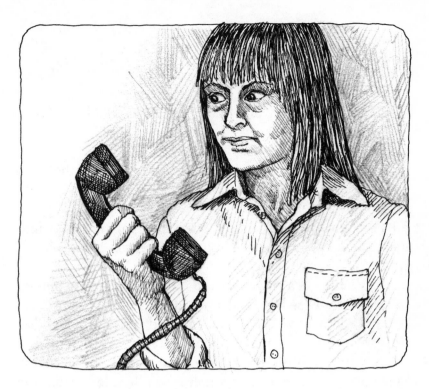

"That so? Maybe it's just slash burning."

"Well, I think I should find out."

"Yeah, I guess so. How's everything up your way? Had any rattlers up there this summer?"

"Uh, listen, I don't mean to be rude, but. . . ." The sun turns blood-colored, the smoke drifts toward our meadow. Minutes on, I get through to our ranger.

"This is Joan, and there's a fire west of us, about three miles."

"That so? Haven't had any reports."

"Well, I'm reporting. It looks like it's spreading fast." Click. A new voice. "That you, Charlie?"

"No, this is Ed."

"Well, hiya, Ed, I was trying to get ole Charlie. How's everything over your way?"

"Same as always," says Ed.

"Hey, Ed, remember me, Joan, and the fire?"

"Who's this?" asks the Charlie caller.

"Dammit, it's Joan, and I'm trying to report a fire. . . ."

"That so, where's it at?"

My jaw is clenched. "*Ed?*"

"Ummm," Ed muses. "Well, I'll have one of the boys mosey over and take a look-see. How's everything up on the mountain?"

"About to go up in flame," I snarl, banging the phone into its cradle. I am rude. I am uppity. I will never learn country ways.

We should get a citizen's band radio for when the phones fail, we are advised by their myriad owners. No thank you. A young hunter was shot last fall and it took his buddies forty-five minutes to make their way, on the emergency channel, through the Old Buddy C.B. chatter. Furthermore, I haven't the time to learn a whole new illiterate lexicon. We should get a horse for when the roads are immobilized, we are advised by their myriad owners. As much as I'd delight in a horse for a friend, we barely break even feeding our goats and flocks. At least motor vehicles, for all their vulnerability, don't eat hay and grain when they're not being driven. We should move closer to civilization, we are advised by the faint of heart. They might have something there. But the new location would have to have an eighty-mile view, an old apple orchard, a piney woods large enough to get lost in, a tumbling creek at its border. . . .

That's the trouble when roots are put down. They cling to the fabric as though their lives depended on it. And sometime when I wasn't looking, their sap flowed into mine.

Apostrophe VI

98° in the Shade

"I am going to go back to California, shut all my windows and turn on the air conditioning," she says. The thermometer on the shaded porch says 98. Waves of heat shimmer up from the parched meadow to the airless hill's crest, parched heat invades every cranny. She fans herself with a paper in the dark pool of our parlor. "I swear I'm going back tomorrow if this doesn't let up."

In consolation, I offer iced tea, in sympathy lie to her that I feel a breeze rising, that the weather report promised a cooling trend. "Just wait," I beg, "one more day." She is my longest-time, truest friend, here on her annual visit, and this record August heat wave threatens to steal our remaining few precious days.

Mike comes in from his workshop, his face flushed brick-red. "Too damned hot to work out there," he says, plopping into a chair.

"Did you get the lock mended?" I ask between his fannings.

"Nah, it'll have to wait until evening. It's over 100 out there."

Friend's child slams the back door, comes in and slumps onto the stool. Sweat streams from his pores, he is panting. "It's too hot to play," he wails. "Mom, I'll *die* without a cold soda."

The dogs whine at the door, their tongues hanging like pink rags. My heart softens and I let them in. They splay across what room is left on the floor, heaving grateful and terminal sighs. The corpse-like cats barely give them the bat of an eye. I rise and make my way through the bodies, thinking how the parlor could pass for a morgue. In the kitchen, I make a fresh pitcher of tea for the inert behind me, then saunter outdoors to take the wash from the line. Bees buzz lazily and a hummingbird darts from a hollyhock to check out my mission. That done, I march down to the garden to parcel out dribbles of water to the thirsty rows. The sun beats on my flesh and scours each weed shadow. Good weather for play. I aim an unthrifty squirt at the hoppers, and the air comes alive with their indignant circus. The toad peers out from a wilted leaf to survey the commotion. I settle beside him, hoping to pass the time of day, but before I can get out "Nice weather," he blinks and retreats. Doesn't anyone share my pleasure at this rare, Saharan day?

My friend has been harping fondly on the previous August when her visit was swathed in thick sweaters, and cold rain rounded each day, cheating the hill of its brightness and my blood of its seasonal bounding. Mike joins her, harkening back to how he was able to cut winter wood then, and what prime chore weather the unlikely chill made. I only remember my cursing the dull pewter skies, and the stove lit to make evenings bearable.

I come up from the garden through the meadow, gathering dry weeds for a late summer bouquet. The seed heads are copper-colored, the stalks palest gold. They'll look nice in the parlor, brighten it like a shaft of sunlight, warm its shadows. They will enhance the shrine of this August I alone bask under.

At the back door, I find Mike clutching his hand. "Ooww,

damned yellow jacket got me," he bellows. "This is all I need on top of this heat!"

I drop the bouquet and rush inside to get the baking soda. At the sink, my friend is splashing cool water over her face. Her son at the table gulps a soda as though it were arctic air. "How can you *bear* it out there?" she demands, "And you're not even sweating!"

Grabbing the baking soda, I mumble, "It's nice, I feel great."

Her son stops his sucking and stares. In his eyes, I am a monster, impervious, obviously, to even the fires of hell. I'm not sure my friend trusts my sanity either.

After treating Mike's hand, I send friend and son off to the lake for a reviving swim. Now, if I could just get this wounded patient out of the house, I could bake up a batch of cookies and treat everyone to a teaparty in the sundowning slip of the day. But there's no hope for it, he is back in the parlor, glaring at the site of his undoing. I pour a tumbler of tea and take it to the porch. Temperature 99 now, the heavy air humming and lovely. I raise my glass and toast the mirage where our meadow back awhile lay.

Let them all swelter and scowl, let friends return to their weather levellers and the creatures pant after each shade. What they consider a heat wave is the closest I reckon I'll get, in this fickle vale, to the beaten-gold heaven I beg.

The Cabin,

An Immobile Home

The farmhouse, full of years and family histories, sits on a
rise above the creek road. Its peaked roof is stout, its front
stoop sturdy. Beside its south wall in spring daffodils grow.

A young city couple bought the place a few years ago.
They came out on occasional weekends for a taste of country,
swept the rooms of dead flies and mouse droppings and then,
for fun, drove their matching motorcycles up and down the
dirt lanes and hillsides. They often said how they envied us
in our life-style, admired our courage. They meant to do the
same, some day, they said, but had to work a few more years.
Farming took money, and the old place needed a world of improvement. The wife made curtains for its windows, an ab-
stract pattern. The old windows looked amazed. Then over
one winter, the water froze and the pipes busted. The kitchen
floor began to sag. We drove by one day and saw a FOR SALE
sign tacked to the fence, below where the daffodils grow.

A few months later, the sign was gone and there was a new
car in the driveway. Curious, we stopped and knocked on
the door. A pleasant, middle-aged woman greeted us and set
down her broom. Her husband was about to retire, she told
us, and they'd be settling here soon. Wasn't this a lovely old

farmhouse, I said. I'd always loved its shape and simplicity. We-e-ll, it needed a lot of work, they thought, so much that they'd about decided to tear it down and replace it with a mobile home. I bit my tongue to hold back its leaping and made a hasty exit. But the old house still had some years in it, for some weeks later the FOR SALE sign returned. Another family eventually bought it, but now they too are thinking of selling. I cross my fingers again for its survival, pray someone will love the big kitchen, the steep, narrow stairs, the daffodils.

When we moved here, there stood on one corner of the valley town the relic of an old hotel. Though its wooden siding hadn't seen a paintbrush in decades, a simple dignity clothed its frame. It was easy to picture its former inhabitants rocking on the screened veranda, fanning themselves, watching the empty street for kernels of easy palaver, and ladies in sweeping skirts mincing down its creaking stairs. But one day in town we found in its place a heap of smoking rubble. The townfolk didn't seem to mind, declared it had been an eyesore anyway. Before our next supply run, a mobile home was planted in its place, tan aluminum, two doors up from the pink Assembly of God. Almost everyone thought it was an improvement.

A few miles west of our mountain, above a winding dirt road, another homestead sits, weather-worn, boarded, peak-roofed like ours. The young family who owns it lives in the mobile home set in its front yard. The house is a shambles, they explain, would take an age to repair.

Down the river, up the valley, they sprout, the glittering pastel boxes, their underpinnings modestly skirted, their flat roofs reflecting the sky. Some have sheltered porches, a few boast picket fences with flowers bedded behind. Those belonging to more thoughtful inhabitants are concealed behind

boulders or trees. And the old homesteads sit idle, their windows agape, their footworn porches sagging.

Why, I once asked a wise neighbor, why don't they repair the old places or, lacking that enterprise, build something simple and new? "Too expensive," she answered, what with the cost of lumber and fancy fixtures. "Besides, those old places don't come with plumbing and all that newfangled frippery."

Frippery, a good term for the matching avocado stove-fridge-washer, the plastic imitation marble sink and commode, the wall-to-wall sculptured carpets and olefin parlor suites, the goldtone light trees and ersatz coach lanterns. And the dwellers go through their days, their lives, touching nothing that breathes, no object that speaks of the earth they were born to and will finally embrace.

I admit we were fortunate. The shell of our sixteen-by-twenty cabin still stood on our hillside when we bought this land. It took the two of us, with the help of an occasional sainted friend, merely three months to make it livable and weather-worthy. Its repair and rebuilding, using wood bought from the local mill and materials scrounged from dumps and second, third, fourth hand shops, cost but a fraction of the sum a modest mobile home begs. We lived in its hand-hewn, gently refurbished space for three years comfortably, feeling at *home*. When we added, with blood, sweat and boards, our twenty-by-twenty-four kitchen/bath, at a cost of less than $2000, we felt we'd been graced with a castle. The old shiplapped walls of what is now our parlor are weather-stained, knot-holed, smoke-coated. I like to rub my hand over them sometimes, feel the bulge here, the gouge there, the patched place where the first homesteader misjudged. Their wood is close kin to the trees nearby; their fabric has become second skin. There's that spot of blood on the beam where I, helping lift it, smashed my finger, and the dent on the floor where the goats pranced before the walls were raised, and that crack in the door frame is where we coaxed the Great Majestic through to the kitchen. Small wounds, to remind us; love bruises.

The stringent land use planning laws in this state do us proud. Our environmental officials are awfully fussy about such things as septic tanks and parcel sizes. Before anyone sells land in these parts, he must inform the county powers of his intentions and get their approval of what he means to do with the place, so that the county can assure the area's continued agricultural base. Plans for a single vacation cabin cause consternation, and settlement on a spread of less than forty acres is highly suspect. They don't bat an eyelash at mobile homes, though. That's progress and, well, there aren't many who have the money to build from scratch.

Four years ago, a friend hand-fashioned a vacation chalet on our east forty. With running tap water, electricity, a sleeping loft, woodstove and weather-proofing—all anyone needs for home comfort—it cost him less than your average family car—and that included his beveled glass window panes, antique oak doors and a charming privy. Another friend is this year constructing a two-story log home for his family from the wood on his land and materials unearthed in village dumps. He has found there more repairable woodstoves than he can use, and eviscerates discarded freezers for their insulation. While they build, the family lives in an old trailer, to which they mean, when the log house is done, to give a proper wake. We plan to attend. I can think of no greater joy than to see a cookie-cutter tin dwelling lowered into the earth which it blighted. Gimcrackery is bad enough in the city; plunked against great sweeps of God's country, it becomes mockery.

It's the way of all flesh, it seems, to opt for the easy, the instant. You can't blame them, those primed by the pre-mixed, factory made all. Yet I do, churlishly, from the shelter of our dear-in-all-but-funds cabin, and wonder what *home* has come to convey. If assembly line fabrication is where the heart is, can human robots be far behind?

The only box you'll catch *my* being in will be built of simple pine.

The Craft That Cut
Those Holes So True

The first privy I ever met belonged to a roaring mining camp in the northern wilds. A fly-by-night shack, its boards faltered in the slightest breeze, and there were enough cracks between them to encourage the entertainment of all the camp's snickering spies. One look at the outfit and I packed my shovel to the woods, where only bears and snakes spied on my toilet, and that from a genteel distance.

Another, later time, we made camp on a high knoll above California's Death Valley, setting up our outdoor home among the flattened shacks and trash heaps of a long-abandoned town. An outhouse was the one structure that still stood, buffeted by gritty wind and hellish weather, held to a cliff's edge by some force no sense could fathom. Peering inside while clinging for dear life to its shell, I could look through the hole and see all the way to the valley's distant floor. For fun, I dropped a rock down the maw, then listened for a desert's eternity to its avalanching bound. In the aftermath of silence, I could only hang my head in respect for the brave souls and true who had disburdened themselves in such a precarious aerie.

I've crossed paths with some good ones in my time, too.

One at the end of a cabin-strewn trail in the nethers of Nevada was as clean as a wooden whistle and so solidly comfortable as to invite daydreams and knothole studies. Another, tucked under I forget whose guarding pines, smelled pleasantly of mushrooms . . . that rich, loamy smell that rises when you dig for wigglers or worts.

But such evaluations were, in those easy years, purely academic. There was always the civilization of two well-furbished, flush-toileted, hot and cold running, tubbed and showered, plush-carpeted rooms of convenience at home to return to, rooms of Pompeian grandeur and consoling familiarity, rooms where one could bless from one's pooled throne this brave new world that hath such plumbing in it, given the contrasts. We even thought for a time of installing a bidet, nursed dreams of the continental flair it might add to our ablutions.

What we ended up with isn't even a rustic cousin. Settling into our new home that first faraway June gave us four months to make the place winter-worthy, to build the structures for the flocks we took in, for the tools and the wrack of our city lives we'd toted a thousand miles. But with a sense of values, the first building we put up was the outhouse. Electricity we could do without for the time being, and hauling buckets of water from the springs was pioneer adventure. But we would, we determined early, have a comfortable shrine for our bodies' daily rites, a room conducive to reflection and renovation, a fortress safe from wood ticks slavering for blood.

The site was chosen with no less deliberation than the lithic architects took in plotting Stonehenge: a hillside perch below the pear thicket, far enough from living quarters to avoid air pollution, yet close enough for convenience, given a touch of foresight and the exercise of mind over matter. Once a commodious hole was dug, the peak-roofed one-holer went up in a trice. While the wood ticks mourned their loss, we graced the bare walls with favored sketches, a Persian hanging, a candle lantern; a braided rug went on the floor, and on the shelf, a wishbook for authenticity. The little house's mien was by this time so cozy we had to draw straws to see who would be first to grace its boards.

It's served for seven years now, and I wouldn't trade it for a world of plumbing. It's the best place on the farm for sky studying and bird watching. The goats join me there each morning, squeezing cozily between the dogs and companionable cats. Once in a while, when the creature crowd threatens all comfort, or when an unexpected truck toils up the hill in

full view of the building's tenant (and vice versa), we consider hanging a door on the thing. But we never have. It would inhibit sky study and bird watch. It might even muffle the creek's music, which climbs the meadow to the outhouse doorsill.

Oh, I'll admit it took a bit at first to stop reaching for the flush handle. And late-night trips were sometimes spooky, when strange sounds whispered by the wall, or the flashlight beam caught a pair of eyes gleaming from the brush nearby. One night in particular, after being nearly knocked off the path by a careening deer, I swore I'd invest in a chamber pot to avoid such darkling dangers. But morning light made my fright foolish. Besides, I thought, far better the deer than a need for Roto-Rooter or a shelf of Sani-Flush.

Then there was the day one of the dogs, bored with mere bones, discovered the roll of toilet paper set neatly beside the hole. We returned from town to find the meadow, the orchard, each weed and every stump festooned. The roll has ever since been hidden under a bowl, and woe to the user who forgets to cover it.

Along with its beauty and utility, the outhouse, we find, offers another boon. It's a sort of litmus paper for city visitors. If a guest grouches, or forgets to follow the instructions to the letter—"Utilize ash bucket freely, stash toilet paper, leave lid up in winter to avoid frost and down in summer to foil flies"—or if he finds his very functions threatened by such primitive style, better he should find a nice motel, one that sports a pastel, plastic-seated, modestly partitioned commode. We've even found it difficult to communicate with anyone who can't find a place in his heart (and vicinity) for our homely Chic Sale. And if said guest's sins mount and his stay appears eternal, a hint that he might help with the annual hole-cleaning dispatches him painlessly. (Actually, the chore's not too distasteful. Liberal additions of wood ashes and sawdust make a decent humus of the night soil, a stuff that, buried, urges the old apple trees to youthful vigor.)

But nothing is perfect. I've yet to hear the most rockribbed outhouser praise its winter virtues. Like the January mornings when the icicles hang swordlike from the eaves, and you know the wooden seat will be frost-crusted. Or the blizzard-driven February nights when you find a snow sculpture where the faithful hole should be. Or chilly dawns when you vie with your outhouse mate over who will be the first to melt the rime, courting chilblains to the bared anatomy.

Yet always, bundled and trussed to the hairline in scarves and jackets, we wend our driven ways down the icy path, thinking of pioneers and Admiral Byrd and better days. And during the visit, made as brief as necessity allows, we venture the surmise: When the seat doth thaw, can spring be far behind?

Visitors to our facilities these recent days wonder aloud why we don't install a septic tank and hook up our bathroom's toilet, installed in a rush of cosmetic virtue two years back. We might, we tell them dreamily, someday. How civilized can you *get*, we think privately, and where would the indoor cats find their drinking water, and where would I put my armsful of summer bouquets? But the hardest sacrifice of all would be of the creek music and the morning robin's call on the outhouse sill.

Some folks, I understand, wile away the time of their toilette with reading matter, to keep up with the world. Mine, commodiously viewed, lies at my feet, privy to the meadow's soliloquy.

Godliness, My Eye

A few months into downhome life, I started having this dream. In it, I'd find myself immersed in a grand marble bathtub awash with perfumed bubbles and steam. Soaking deep in its vapors, I would wile away hours in the very lap of liquid luxury.

Funny, how baths in the city used to be mere dunkings to be gotten through in the common course of a day, how even showers back then were pedestrian, of no event. Once we'd settled into our country cabin, our one chill, spring-fed spigot made them the stuff of which dreams were made.

It's not that I would have bartered our wondrous spring, our chipped enamel sink and home-plumbed tap for any of the city luxuries in that distant cosmos. Just the taste of our mountain water was and still is sublime, after years of the chlorinated urban stuff. Furthermore, the dirt we accrue here, unpolluted and polyunsaturated, doesn't require a daily purge, nor does being a mile and a half from the nearest neighbor make us fret over whether we're apt to offend.

Luckily, we had years of experience in making do at dry desert camps before we moved to our simple homestead. Our five-gallon water jug followed us faithfully on each city escape, and with proper chariness its contents could be made to last for a number of days. Sand worked wonders on dirty pots and pans, and many were the canals and waterways we dunked our bodies into for hasty renewal. I've a chill memory too of a shampoo accomplished in a snow-fed mountain stream one early spring, and that I couldn't feel the locus of my head for hours after.

One of the things Mike built early into our first summer was a primitive solar shower. Outdoors, of course, the cabin being in disrepair, plunk against the side of the shed where the sun beat through the day. A twenty-gallon drum was set up on a frame of aluminum foil reflectors, with a simple spigot for the shower head. Duckboards underfoot were its sole luxury. No walls, no modest shower curtain. Such accoutrements seemed unnecessary since but one or two rigs a day passed the meadow's bottom, and their passengers would have needed binoculars to see all the way up to the al fresco bather.

Yet invariably, the minute I'd bare my body to the sun-warmed (to near-scalding, if the day's temperature rose over 90°) water, a telltale of dust would rise from the road, and my demure mind would race with visions of saucer-eyed randies slavering over my flesh. "Looky there, Billy-Jim, a nekked lady, ooh boy . . ." Or worse, once I got totally lathered up, a snowman of soapsuds, the stream of overhead water would turn to trickle, then drips, then . . . "Mike, dammit, you forgot to fill the barrel again your last turn!" And Mike would come running sheepishly, toting the hose like a freshman fireman, to refill the thing post-haste, to flood me with spring-chill water, to wash off the suds and give me goosebumps the size of golfballs all over my shivering frame.

But clean, oh how good clean felt after a day in the mulch-dusty garden, after hours of cleaning animal droppings out of the cabin's floor boards or tearing off rotting roof shingles.

Summer sun, like all blessings, passes, and with autumn's frosty mornings and scant daylight hours, the shower drum

barely luke-warmed. Further, as soon as one stood under its
tepid water, a breeze would scud up the meadow to blast the
wet body and cause one to grab towels and clothes, soapy or
no, and race for protective shelter. Finally, sadly, we emptied
the barrel, bid it a grateful farewell and got out the shiny new
galvanized washtub. It looked much smaller than it had in the
store.

We had, by this time, winterproofed and furnished the
cabin to our satisfaction. One corner, next to the closet
where everything from soup through grain to nut bolts was
stored, we'd made into a kitchen, replete with Ashley, the
Great Majestic, the minuscule sink; a rose-patterned square
of linoleum covered the floor. What with the logs stacked for
fires and the baskets of kindling and the trash and garbage
containers and the humpback trunk full of towels and clothing, there was barely enough room in the middle to set bathing utensils. Oh, it was cozy. But the first time I christened
the bathing arrangement, I ended up with my hair soap-
grungy and the tub awash on a flooded linoleum sea. Clearly,
the procedure needed refining.

Within weeks, I had it down to an art. Herewith, my bath
recipe. As in all recipes, the user will add his own improvements according to taste . . . and in this case, size. I can't imagine how a Bill Walton, say, would manage. But then truly
outsize people would probably build bigger shelters in the
first place.

Bath ingredients:

1 galvanized steel tub, at least twenty inches in diameter
1 seven-quart pot (the canning kind is good)
1 eight-quart cooking vessel
1 modest dishpan

A passel of newspapers
Washcloth, towel, non-detergent soap and shampoo (You
don't want a sea of suds necessitating endless rinsings.)

Directions

Fill to almost brimful the canning pot and cooking vessel.
Place on high heat. (The wood cookstove will take up to an
hour to get properly hot. The bonus here is that the bathing
area will get all warm and snug in the process, driving potential invaders of privacy to cooler regions.) As the waters
reach the steaming point, spread newspapers about on the
floor and place tub in their middle. Place dishpan inside the
tub, set towels and soaps within easy reach. Pour 1/3 of lar-
ger pot's steaming water into dishpan, add enough cold water
for shampoo comfort. Kneel as though to pray, dunk head,
soap hair and scrub away. This done, wring out hair, throw
towel around head, dump soapy dishpanful into sink. Refill
dishpan with another 1/3 of hot water, adding cold again
as before. Rinse hair in this, with a dash of vinegar to help
chase suds. Pour out water and repeat process one more time.
Do not throw out this third rinse water! Instead, pour it into
galvanized tub, add enough hot water from second vessel for
bathing comfort. Pour remaining hot water into dishpan and
add enough cool water to make comfortable. Snuggle dishpan right up to tub.
    Your bath, madame or sir, is ready.

    Being longish of limb, I found the best position was to sim-
ply sit my gluteal parts in the tub with my legs dangling over
the edge. There I soaped and scrubbed away, and once spot-
less, stood up in said tub for the rinsing. The latter was accomplished by dunking the washcloth repeatedly into the

dishpan of clear water and splashing it over the streaming form. (This is where the carpet of newspapers came in handiest.) A quick rub with a dry towel, wallowing in the heat of the blessed woodstove, and I felt pure enough to enter heaven.

Though the mop-up was anti-climactic, it too took some thought. Rather than heft the full tub onto the porch for dumping, tempting a chill in the process, I emptied the dishpan first, then dipped the tub water out with it into the sink. The wet newspapers were forthwith rolled to dry by the stove, where they made a good start for the next morning's fire.

One of the pleasanter aspects of such simple baths was their recyclability. If I wasn't too dirty going in—and it's .hard to get terribly sullied when snow covers every inch of the earth—Mike often followed me into the tub. It's only good country tradition, the cleanest going first, and there is a companionable feeling about flesh washed in shared waters.

Though the tub in the honest-to-God bathroom we've added is neither massive nor marble, it has dragon-clawed feet and room enough to loll to Elysium. Sometimes when I'm soaking therein, I think back to that single spigot and the pots steaming atop the woodstove. It makes a person positively sentimental. Maybe this winter, I tell myself, I'll rescue the galvanized tub from under the porch and relive my lost ceremony. Maybe, I tell myself, sinking deeper into the sudsy water, this winter . . . or next. . . . Right now all I know is that whoever said water was not the natural habitat of humanity didn't bark up *my* tree.

Although I've never been one to put much stock in electric appliances, having been reared with every newfangled contraption to come down the pike, one birthday present that will live in memory for my country lifetime is the fifty-gallon hot water heater Mike gave me on my forty-somethingth celebration. Though we mean someday to build a solar assist, and though we still use the outdoor solar shower the minute summer lives up to its name, that lovely tank, be-ribboned for the occasion, was gift beyond compare. Luckily, for conservation's sake, our galvanized tub days broke those compulsive bathing habits which the makers of deodorant bars and gaseous pit sprays dun into us ad ridiculum. The water heater remains set at a moderate 130°, and we plot our baths hours ahead with the same sort of anticipation others feel before a night on the town.

"Can we use your bathtub?" a few guests are emboldened to ask. Before a decision is made, we scrutinize their elbows and the backs of their ears and weigh the request as soberly as high-bench judges. If the beggar doesn't realize by then that a hot bath is not a gift to be taken lightly, he has a black hole where his soul should be. Furthermore, it appears to us the height of ill manners for a guest to be wafting cleaner than his hosts choose to be.

On the other hand, I do admit to a cultural aversion to dirty attire. Grease spots could demean a saint in my eyes, and a soiled neckband makes my stomach churn. While sheets, socks and outer garments can be aired for a day to recapture freshness (a trick I learned from an Italian friend familiar with water shortage), pure grime demands pure soap and water. During the years we lived with our one cold water spigot, there were times when I despaired of ever catching up with the mountains of laundry. To stay as pristine as my spirit demanded, I found myself devoting every third day to the boiling of clothes on the stove, the pumping of sheets and jeans with my toilet plunger, the rubdubbing of knuckles raw on my de Sadian scrubboard. Then one holy day, a neighbor offered us her discarded washing machine. An automatic.

"I've nowhere to put it," I wailed, scanning the crammed-cornered cabin.

"We'll take it," Mike said. "I'll make do."

Bless his making-do heart. Where the contraption ended was on boards outside our kitchen washbasin, exposed to the elements, and a scar on the natural beauty of the old cabin boards. And lovely, lovely, compared to the painful nobility of constant hand-laundering and a cabin that felt like a sauna every third day. There are times when one must say to the esthetic and pioneer spirit, "Bug off."

Mike's making do was simply to drill a hose-sized hole beneath the sink (plugged with a cork when not in use) through which I could snake the hose, attached at one end to my indoor spigot and at the other to the machine's orifice. Voila! Insta-clean laundry, at the drop of a rush of cold water, liquid soap and a dollop of sudsy ammonia. Cold water didn't work quite as famously as the steaming sort on imbedded grime, true, but its bonus was that nary an item of clothing was shrunk for over two years, a record for one who has toted a carton of lilliputian wool sweaters through her scatterbrained lifetime.

The faithful machine now sits in our laundry cubicle, hooked up to the hot water tank, its years of weather exposure having made no dent in its function.

Most of our farmer neighbors, who now possess dryers, ask why I still hang my clothes on the line. It's hard to explain that I love the sound of their flapping on breezy days, the fresh smell of them taken down (oh, pungent bundles!), love even the feel and design of wooden clothespins. They wouldn't understand how, in the city, where we retrieved our weekly wash neatly packaged from a Chinese family, I used to stand stock-still for whole minutes, my eyes lifted to a banner of clothes strung out from a tenement window, how I envied the sturdy housekeepers who could sleep on air-scented pillows, pile their baskets with sun-blessed vestments and feel crisply right with their world.

I think of that now, in midwinter, tugging frozen garments from the line with icy fingers, hanging them in the loft to drip and steam and grudgingly dry, rubbing my hands back to life over the fire. I think of modern man's cleanliness penchant, of adulthood's strictures. I think, in my fairweather famine, Godliness my eye!

In Sickness
or in Health

Like the lungers of old, we came to the countryside for our health. It wasn't our bellows that needed mending so much as Mike's mounting blood pressure and the seeds of an executive ulcer. City pressures, stress symptoms—his were the classic models. That I fared a bit better, I lay to my female sturdiness and a lifelong love for long walks. Lacking woods or country lanes, no hill, alley or park in the city went unexplored. Frequent forays into health foods might have helped too, if they hadn't been largely attempts to balance massive splurges of Hersheys with infusions of smokes and coffee.

A few months into farm life, Mike's blood pressure simmered down and the locus of his duodenum no longer throbbed. While he had to pull his belt in by two inches, I added pounds of hale flesh to my bony frame. I've a notion that the cause of these improvements was that our bodies, given worthy outdoor exercise and wholesome food, found their natural balance, that we became physically what our birthright had meant us to be.

Living quietly, simply, close to the earth has, over the years, put me in closer touch with my constitution. The communication between mind and flesh is no longer circuitous, nor apt to be detoured by the contagious distractions urban living contains. The psyche's structure not being prone to instant alchemy, this new awareness took a long time to brew.

During our earlier winters, when the snow drifted to the doors and the temperature plummeted, we caught cold or were struck by flu symptoms beyond our just share. Medical wisdom has it that these diseases are viruses carried from one person to another. Yet here we were on a weathered-in mountain, out of touch for weeks with kith, kin or neighbor. Each time we took to the aspirin and Vicks bottles, we speculated as to how this could be. Surely the most virulent bug couldn't make its way through subfreezing weathers all the way from the valley to invade our unwary veins; and surely good food and wood-chopping and backpacking supplies up the meadow, and snowshoeing and tending our creatures were healthy exercise.

Yet such slumps into paltry infirmities continued until, during our fourth winter, I was flattened by a case of pneumonia. It had been a dreary season, with long stretches of stone-grey skies and a chill that ate to the bone. Our financial worries lay heavy on us, and it was too cold outdoors to lighten them with winter play. Day upon day, my usually ebullient mood dimmed until it was as lifeless as the weather's, as heavy as the layers of snow. And then I got sick, deathly so.

In the still center of this illness, the one I was certain was terminal, we were snowed away from humanity with no means under heaven of reaching a doctor. To make matters worse, when Mike tried to phone for advice, he found the line dead to the world. I hadn't enough vitality even to curse my fading fate. The long nights were the worst, dark hours of struggling to breathe, to lift the invisible boulder from my drowning bellows. Trying to find something to hang onto

for dear life, I asked Mike to read to me. He got out the *Narnia Chronicles* and read aloud into the nights. Each phrase was a branch, in the tide that engulfed me, to grasp. When his voice faltered or slurred with sleep, I begged him, with what breath I could muster, to read on . . . and on. And he did, for more nights than I can remember, until the tide receded and I knew I'd see the next spring.

Some weeks into my recovery, we were able to beat our fifty-mile route through melting snow to the doctor. He gave me some antibiotics and the discouraging counsel that I'd not likely feel healthy again until summer. Forthwith, I obeyed. (Oh, revered doctors, be warier of your heavy words than of your nostrums!)

The slow process of regaining my vitality left me vast time to ponder, and it came to me haltingly that I had probably caused my own body's malfunction. In allowing my mind to fall prey to worries and weathers, I had invited the contagion to spread into the core of my vessel. With this new recognition of the interdependence of every molecule, I determined, as far as was possible, to protect myself from my own further victimization.

But even with this vow tucked into my psyche, I figured I had better give myself and Mike every chance. Though we'd always been physically sturdy, our distance from medical aid and our winter conditions left small room to gamble. In retrospect, it was a wonder we'd made it so well this far, with our earlier city habits of quick cups of coffee grabbed on the way out the door, lunchtimes often ignored, and dinners taken more often than not in restaurants or at clamorous parties. Sleep then was something you wrestled with between the last late night hurrah and the morning's sprint to the office. It made my shoulders tight just remembering.

A complete change of eating habit was the first easy step into country living, one that was taken almost overnight. Our chickens' brown eggs looked so earthy, the yolks so upright and golden, and the garden vegetables tasted like nothing had tasted before. And there were our burgeoning appetites, hungers we hardly recognized in their stirrings, nurtured by long hours of labor in the glass-bright air and our constant up and downhill directions. So eggs for breakfast became a new habit, and later our goats' milk was added. Dinners were a pleasure to concoct from our garden's treasure, with a bit of meat from an animal we knew to have enjoyed an undoctored prime.

One habit, though, I never could cotton to was the big midday meal. The farm-learning hours slipped away too quickly for me to note the sun's telltale position or harken to my breakfastful belly.

"It's two o'clock, and I'm starving," from Mike.

"Oh, uh, there's some cheese in the fridge."

"*Cheese?* What sort of lunch is *that?*"

"Well, if you'll wait til I get this last row planted. . . ."

But after the seeds were settled, there was the mulch to lay, and the chickens to feed, and a bird I'd never seen might flicker into the pines, tempting me to follow. And before I knew it, the sun would be setting and the animals heading home.

"I forgot. Did you find yourself some lunch?"

"Yup, heated the leftover stew. What's for dinner?"

"Leftover stew."

Mike gave up after a while, and resigned himself to fixing his lunch without a word to me of the hour. Which was fine. Eat when you're hungry, I say, not when the hands of the clock stir your innards.

People on this side of the world eat too much anyhow, a fact proven by the glut of fad diets and the boosterism of weight-loss clubs. Food seems to fill some want they're at pains to identify, some unmet human yen. I have yet to see a chubby deer or a gross rabbit; and a bird would never get off the ground if he took a page from man's habit. Animals seem better in tune with their natures, don't fill their bellies with food to satisfy hungers that have nothing to do with their nutritive needs. At least it's not common. We do have an uncommon goat, I admit, who is fonder of food—any food—than she should be. But once she became a mother, her youthful chubbiness disappeared in some mysterious leveling process. Maybe her misplaced hungers were for kids of her own, or maybe motherhood somehow adjusted her appestat. I like to think she simply matured and sensed that to keep up with her bounding children she had better be fleet of foot and sleek of form. Would that her human counterparts could act out of such wise self-counsel.

"How do you stay so thin?" It's a refrain I've heard through my years, most often from frustrated weight-watchers.

"Inheritance," I answer, only half truthfully. If I were more bluntly honest, I would add that I don't sit around on my geezer, that I am fond of *doing*, and that I view edibles more as fuel for my energies than reward or consolation. But because I do tend to forfeit meals for other pleasures, or simply lose track of their need, I sneak into my system each day a few healthy concoctions. Like my Orange Milk Shake:

Orange Milk Shake

To one quart milk (goat's, preferably), add 2/3 cup concentrated orange juice (powdered or whole), 2 tbsp. honey, 1 tsp. vanilla, 1/4 cup each brewer's yeast and granular lecithin and powdered milk and bone meal. Blend or beat vigorously.

A glass of this each morning sets me up for the most wintery day. Further, to have handy for each batch of bread, cookies, pancakes, I make up a formula of the brewer's yeast-lecithin-bone meal-powdered milk combination, adding a handful each of wheat germ and bran. These ingredients make little difference in the taste of the product, but they do assure a fine fettle.

It's passing strange, the effect farm life has had on my tastebuds. Though a day seldom lapsed in the city that I didn't gobble a candy bar, king size, or a fistful of oreos or a banana split with the works, my countrified gullet soon lost its craving for such goop. It might simply be that wholesome food fills all my crannies, or that more balanced eating offers the energy my body once sought in sweets. Or maybe I've fostered an overweening fondness for the handiwork of our cherished soil. Whatever the reasons, my innards are grateful. I'd be hard-pressed to run a farm on the fuel of chocolate twinkies.

But hold. Lest I be classed as yet another nutrition groupie, I must make a confession. Though our larder boasts its measure of sprouts and yogurt and binsful of fresh vegetables in season, I still weaken at odd times of the year and fantasize the savor of a Big Mac or double deck cone. "What can we bring?" friends heading out from the city inquire. "Junk food," I beg. If there's a jot of human kindness in them, they comply, and I stash the gutless greasies in a corner of the cupboard for the dourest of days, or an hour in any season when nothing goes right and I yearn for just the smallest swallow of imitation, agent-orange dyed, reconstituted, hydrogenated hemlock.

Nobody's perfect. I bet Adelle Davis even sneaked down a hot dog sometimes.

You'd think a farmer's regime such as ours would provide enough exercise to keep the body tuned to near perfection, that climbing a 45-degree hill from the garden, coop, goat barn to the cabin, and from the cabin to the feed bin and springs would guarantee trusty sinew and sturdy bone.

I thought so for years. I was wrong. Because each season demands different chores than the last, and their weathers limit or expand the amount of exertions, our bodies end up getting inconsistent rewards. For a time, each spring found us feeling like bears emerging from hibernation, musty and stiff and slow to catch up to earth's quickening. And whereas long summer days give us room to work out of doors until eight or nine, winter nights confine us to a battened-up cabin and cheek-to-jowl kinship with the wood stoves. It's enough to make vital organs schizophrenic, particularly those which, like ours, had been shaped in semi-tropical climes.

Not one to sit still for winters' grey lung disease, spring

stiffness or summers' rainy day doldrums, I recently took to the study of practical alternatives. Jogging was the first to cross my mind. (Actually, bicycling held the greatest immediate appeal, but there's not a bike on the market that could make it through the stretches of dust, potholes, rivulets and rockpiles our paths are made of . . . in *good* weather.) So one lovely spring day, I donned my best tennies, took a lungful of air and began my first sprint across the meadow footpath. It wasn't ten seconds before the dogs sat up, took notice and bounded to my side, nipping my heels and leaping all over my person in joyous abandon. Ten more seconds, and I was sprawled on the earth, being licked up a wet storm by my doggy gamesters. Clearly, some private, indoor activity would be the better part of valor.

Dancing—that was the ticket. I would put on a short stack of records and play Fred Astaire, maybe work up to apprentice Isadora. But that notion got almost as short shrift as the original. Our cabin parlor measures sixteen by twenty and brags as many geegaws as an over-endowed museum. The second room, the kitchen, is equally jampacked. And even if I hadn't stubbed my toe with each graceless step, a vigorous shift or swift kick shook the foundations to their very stones. The cabin, though sturdy enough for a century of comings and goings, was poorly provided for balletic leaps. A more minimal form of tune-up would have to do. And lo, it came upon me that nothing is more minimal or salutary than Hatha Yoga. It was a notion sent from Vishnu him (Him?) self.

So I started slowly, as the good books advise, taking fifteen or twenty minutes a day to stretch into the ten basic Yoga positions. Easy. Peaceful, too. And far better than dogged decathalons, except when Mike bounded into the parlor and bumped right into my halfassed lotus. Sniff.

"What smells?"

"Om. Shh. It's Radha's Devotion incense."

"Mmm, smells more like Rosie's whorehouse."

"Shh. Ommm. . . ."

"Hey, could you unwrap yourself and come hold a board for me?"

"Om, damn." It's hard to bliss out around a Taurean workaholic. I did, I confess, feel a bit self-indulgent, taking time out from farm toil. But focusing on one's vessel of flesh has a way of distancing shoulds and have-to's. Before I knew it, I was stealing almost an hour each day for my precious practice, and feeling not selfish at all. Self-*centered*, rather, in the best sense, and so refreshed I could double my chores.

"Why don't you try a bit every day?" I asked Mike at the wood pile, between axe-heftings.

"Me? I get plenty of exercise." Thump, crack. A log bites the dust.

"That's a different kind. Yoga is concentrated, energizing."

"Yeah, well, I'd feel . . . um . . . silly. Besides, I've got to get this wood chopped and the workshop cleaned out, and that chickenyard fence needs mending. . . ."

It's hard to bliss out when you're a New England-reared pragmatist. Hard, too, to find time, even when time is our own creation, in a place where clocks lose their command. Yet ruts are not just city pitfalls. One must not only take care to be physically hale in rural solitude; the head too must be nourished and opened for air. A return to nature, to basics, can be a new beginning. The trip might well lack adventure if the old self rules the way.

A proposal I once read somewhere often comes to my mind, that one could learn much by lying down beside a carrot seedling and watching it grow. Somehow, I've never yet managed such patience. The closest I've come is to take a space of each farm-busy day to be still and observe my own seed-work. Often, a shaft of sunlight pierces the window, a bird chirps from the apple tree. These reminders make more sense of my being than any illusory nostrum might offer or medical wizard advise.

II

I COULD TURN

AND LIVE WITH THE ANIMALS

Reverence for All Life
and a Rifle at the Door

Sometimes I have to wonder if I was cut out to be a farmer at all. It's not that the work isn't rewarding, or the physical demands beyond my energies. It's the judgments, the decisions that must be made about where we fit into nature's balance that try my soul. Our mountain acres had rested untouched for forty years before we made them home. We don't want to tip the balance; we want to become part of this land, not lord over it. But it's not easy, and we have a long way to go.

Loath to kill the lowliest creature, I have been known to beg a potential executioner to spare the life of a fly or cornered mite. In searching my soul for reasons for this empathy, all I've dredged up is one small memory of my engulfing horror when I let three goldfish slip down the drain at a tender age (mine; the fish were well past their prime). Later, my choice of the likes of Schweitzer and Saint Francis as demigods fleshed out some dim but sturdy faith in the sacredness of all forms of life.

One of the reasons we chose this sheltered mountainside

was to be part of the forests' and fields' essence and their creatures' habits, to listen in on the birds' prattle and find woods
tenants unhazarded by human incursion.

And among the first words we heard from our farmer and
woodsman neighbors was "kill."

"You gotta get rid of them porcupines, they'll strip your
trees dead." This from a woodcutter who makes his wages
helping hack whole forests to pulp.

"You heard coyotes? Better get your rifle ready. They
won't leave your flocks any peace."

"Coons? Kill 'em. They're death on chickens."

"Rabbits? They won't leave a stalk standing."

"Grasshoppers? Spread poison. They'll eat your crops to
the ground."

Wildcats, sand rats, robins, sparrows, all were offered
nonchalantly on the altar of practical husbandry. My head
boggled above a sinking heart. If subsistence farming meant
murdering wild fellow creatures to survive, I wanted none
of it. There must be another way.

It took but a season or two to realize that the small farmers
and ranchers in our valley barely eked out an existence with
what they had, that predators meant losses they simply
couldn't afford. They're jolly, decent folks, our neighbors,
and veritable holies when it comes to helping us ex-city
dunces. But when I took issue with their warnings about the
threat our wildlings posed, they winked and grinned, a "just
wait" wisdom on their weathered faces.

During our first summer, nature seemed bent on proving
my trust worthy, offering nary a bug to our vegetable rows.
The orchard's bird families eyed even the strawberries from
a wary distance. The only four-footed beasts who seemed to
dare our inhabited hill were the deer, peering shyly from the
woods' protection and sniffing the newly stirred air. Then

late one sultry August night, a strange snuffling rose from the orchard, accompanied by the sorts of sounds a gruff owl might make. Prying the darkness with flashlights, we lit on a rotund porcupine lumbering up the hill. Meeting him half way, we prodded him with sticks into a handy barrel, where he hid his head in shame, and the next day, hoisted him barrel and all into the pickup for transport to more solitary quarters. A few days later, a pack of coyotes prowled down our hillside, headed directly for the duck pond. We drove them off with ungodly hollers, and it was the last we saw of them or their kin that year. When the first October's hunting season arrived, we sent silent messages to the deer for miles around to take refuge in our hiding places. Something in them must have comprehended, for sisters, cousins, youngsters teemed our forest's corridors, cringing with us at the shattering barrage.

Then it was winter, with its infinite snows. Crisp mornings, we'd swaddle ourselves to our noses to trudge down through the meadow drifts and through the tree paths, tracing creature meanders and harkening to smallest sounds. Deer tracks trafficked everywhere, and here and there, the tiny prints of rabbits. One morning, we came across fist-size cat prints by the creek crossing, and tracked them upward toward a hillside den. I shook off a quiver and looked over my shoulder in a mixture of fear and hope that we might spy this great snow stalker and prove we meant him no harm. But the silence only deepened in the drifted gully, so we turned back, whispering to each other of his need for privacy and our own shaky bravado.

Late spring brought melting snows and the emergence of our buried road. When we could get to town again, the neighbors displayed amazement that we'd wintered over, survived whole. "Better get yourselves some shooting iron," a number of them advised darkly. "Hard winter makes wild critters hungry." We nodded and kept our counsel. There was no point in feeding their judgment of our naïvite.

The second summer proved our Rubicon, a test of our commitment to sharing this space with our simple denizens. Insects, word having gotten around about my garden's banquet, invaded in legion. The seedling cabbages fell first to their eager hungers; I planted more. They moved on to the cauliflower. Next it was beetles, gorging the new potato leaves, then worms, feasting on low-branching tomatoes. I planted and replanted and scraped massed stalks. And swore. I dusted with ashes and poured on garlic tea until the rows were powdery and pungent. And swore. Desperate, we cleaned out the Merc of rotenone, and sprinkled it at every busy corner. I begged the ladybugs and toads to stuff themselves on anything that moved. Grudgingly, the troops finally withdrew . . . at just the time the orchard birds threw caution to the winds and assailed the strawberry patch like ladies at a bargain basement table. Covering the plants with lengths of nylon netting, I promised the birds I'd leave all the fields' wild currants as compensation.

Surprisingly, despite what seemed for a time overwhelming odds, our garden by midsummer took hold, thrived, and promised a hearty harvest. Feeling like a fair-weather friend, I found it in my heart to uncover the remaining strawberries for bird desserts. They had, after all, left more than enough for our palates, and I didn't want them to think their co-tenant a skinflint.

That same year, before even the first sprouts were breaking ground, I found in the chicken coop one morning a wrack of blood and feathers. Chicken remains lay strewn asunder. I counted my flock; two hens missing. I screamed for Mike.

We took the evidence to the nearest neighbor. "Coons,"

she announced. "They leave that kind of mess." Heavy-hearted, we double-fenced the chickens' quarters and screened up each thumb-sized gap in their coop. A week later, I discovered one of the four ducks stone-dead beside her pond. A set of tooth marks pierced her delicate back. The other ducks waddled near to share my mourning, their chorus subdued, then followed me in funereal procession while I carried the remains uphill for burial beneath a pine. "Coyotes," the knowing neighbor told us. "The other ducks must have raised a ruckus and frightened the pack off before they got the rest." It was yet another grave notch in our learning tree.

Our second spring was ushered in by flocks of robins and whole families of porcupines. The vanguard, an infant, we found huddled against the cabin's south wall one April day. He shied in fright at our approach, and at the cats stalking a wise distance away. Though we tried to reassure him, his bristling quills told us he was in no mood to socialize, so we let him be. Surely one tot of a porcupine could do little harm.

Soon the moonlit trees were full of porcupine kin. They peered curiously down from branches at our evening chores, crooned love songs to our open windows through the night. The country pup we'd adopted that season barked fits around the tree trunks when she spied them. They glared back and harrumphed disdain. "Back!" we shouted if she got too close to a descending quill factory, and "Back!" when her curiosity drove her after a scurrying porcupine tail. Though she seemed to sense the hazards and maintain a safe distance, we worried. The best we could do was to hope her yelpings would wreck their nerves and drive them to a quieter shelter. But if there's one quality a porcupine prides itself in, we discovered, it's nerves of steel.

"I'll send Billy up," a neighbor offered, "He loves to shoot

the varmints." We demurred politely, adding, no doubt, to
the lore of our alien ways.

"They're good eatin'," another farmer told us, but we were
suffering enough qualms over occasional chicken slaughter.

By the middle of August, the garden bounty reached full
bloom. While we gorged on rosy tomatoes and crisp greens,
on peas and beans and early corn, on baby potatoes and stripling onions, we licked our chops over the broccoli and cauliflower and squashes yet to come. Then one morning, bent on
a watering tour of the proud rows, I found in the northwest
quarter a no-man's-land. Where yesterday the broccoli and
Brussels sprouts had flourished and the creamy cauliflower
had peeked out of its leaves was tattered waste. Broken stalks
stood bare, trampled leaves lay limp on the ground. I stared
in disbelief until my eyes burned, wondering what beast
could have managed such swift and total ruin. Surely no deer
could have leapt the nine-foot fence, and the sturdy juniper
poles held the wire smack to the ground. The few gophers
the cat hadn't caught yet broached only an occasional root,
and we hadn't seen a rabbit within miles. After a while, Mike
joined me. We stared and swore softly together, then slumped
to the ground. Broccoli was his favorite.

That evening, we posted ourselves on the hillside with
flashlights, our eyes sharp. In no time at all, a bristling lump
emerged from the nearby wood and hunkered toward the
garden. Our friend, the porcupine. With amazing speed for
his kind, he scaled a juniper post like a veteran lineman and
landed in the midst of the garden's remaining board.

"That does it!" Mike declared in the darkness. "We're
going to buy ourselves a rifle." I said not a word, but my heart
beat hollow. How could our home remain a refuge for the
grand and the small if we insisted on dominion, on a weight-
ing of the delicate scale?

Before we had a chance to reach a supply town where the dreadful weapon could be bought, nature played yet another hand. Wakened early one morning by heart-rending howls, we found our pup huddled on the porch, her snout a repository of quills. While I consoled and scolded her in a breath, Mike went for the pliers. The awful hours of the operation drained into afternoon while we took turns holding down the agonized dog and yanking quills one by one. Her muzzle ran blood and she whimpered miserably. When the last quill was pulled, we doctored her wounds and our own as well, for with her pain had come confused rage. The ordeal at last over, she fled behind the woodstove and crouched, trembling, her eyes speaking betrayal. Mangled, exhausted, we dropped onto the porch sill. "Okay," I muttered, "we'll get that cursed gun."

I had turned some dark corner into an alien land.

The gun we ended up with was a modest .22, efficient

enough for quick death to the small and the slow. Sticking it in a corner, we did our best to ignore it. "Be gone!" I shouted into the porcupines' shadows. "Please leave, we don't want a battleground." The old apple branches rustled and I got in reply but a snort.

A few nights on, the dog set to a yapping ruckus under the front yard tree. Mike grabbed the gun from its corner and gruffly ordered me to follow with the flashlight. The porcupine was a big one. Peering down from the leafy thicket, he seemed pathetically courageous in the face of such odds. It took four shots to bring him to earth, and he fell with a sickening thud. When we came back inside, Mike's face was ashen. "I hate this," he muttered. I could only bite my lip and nod.

As summer elapsed, we killed another and another, running out at the dog's barked alert to shoot into a pair of scared eyes caught in my trembling light's beam. As much as we tried to numb our senses, to be mechanical about the deeds, reminding each other this was for the dog's protection, we dreaded increasingly the summer nights' bloody summons. By harvest time, the garden was a porcupine graveyard, the rotting carcasses fertilizing the dwarf fruit trees.

When a series of late summer frosts sent the creatures trundling off to their forest dens, we stuck the tainted rifle out of sight and sighed a sigh of gratitude for verging winter's recess.

Another morning of another spring dawned and I found the chicken coop a mass of blood and savaged bodies. This time the coon had wrought total havoc. Six of my prettiest pullets were torn limb from limb. We scanned the "coon-proof" coop at every corner until we at last spied tell-tale claw marks on the outside wall, and above them, a small space pried open below the chicken wire. "I'm going to get that bastard," Mike vowed through gritted teeth.

I walked slowly back up the hill and stood staring across the meadow to the woods' shades. Nature, benign and bountiful, was also red in tooth and claw. Who was to draw the line? We were accountable for the lives we brought to this place, I reflected; it was our duty to shelter and protect them as best we could. And yet, in the end, though we loved and individualized each of our "owned" creatures, we ourselves killed a portion of those we reared. Wasn't our resentment of this predation part of the same blindness that made the woodsmen rant at porcupine "destruction"? And if we vowed to defend our own, who then was to defend the wild creatures, those who, like us, killed to eat and survive? The happenstance of our refined means of destruction seemed no rationale at all.

A few mornings later, the dog gave a sharp warning bark from the porch. We peered out the window and caught sight, in the high crotch of the apple tree, of a coon's mask, its eyes terrified. Mike went for the rifle. "No!" I shouted, but he strode out the door, intent on his mission. The gunshot sounded before the echo of my own voice had died.

His face was a grim mask when he came back inside, his hands shaking.

"We can't do this any more," I whispered.

He sat down beside me. "What about the chickens and the ducks? And soon we'll have goats and their kids. What if something threatens them?" His words came out hard, and I knew he was as torn as I.

"There's got to be a better way," I mused aloud. "Maybe we'll all just have to take our chances together."

We talked on through the morning, quietly, with long silent spaces between our words. When we were done, Mike hung the rifle silently above the door, too high for my reach, hard even for his. Would there ever be a time we could put it out of sight completely?

A local farmer's son once showed us a lynx pelt he'd skinned out, bragging how he had poached the creature just north of our woods. I stroked the soft fur and whispered to no one, "Shame." We are told the land around us was recently roamed by black bears. "It's better now," the farmers declare. "They put a bounty on 'em. Haven't seen a bear now for, oh, ten years, I'd say." An eagle couple kept house until recently in a tall burnt snag across the creek. When we walked the creek banks, listening to water music and spying for darting trout in the secret pools, they soared screaming overhead, warning us to keep our distance from their aerie. We did, but others might not have. "It's a dirty shame," a farm woman had commented, "that it's illegal to kill them. They're death on chickens and lambs." Remembering our own rifle's dirty business, I could find nothing to say.

Last summer, on the dusty road to town, a ring-necked pheasant crossed our path, while his dusky mate explored the roadside ditch. Excited, I told the next neighbor we met. "Oh, the valley used to be full of them," she said, "but Dutch, over east of here, he loves to hunt 'em. I'm surprised there are any left. Thought he'd done in the whole lot." Oh rainbow-wing, come make your home in our hollows, where we'll honor your being and try to make amends.

Sometimes deep in a winter night, I hear the cougar scream from the rimrocks. An elk bugles from the east draw in the spring. A wolf loped across our hillside one distant grey dawn, and its vision cast a spell on my days. That evening, when I locked up the goats and chickens with wary caution, I pondered for a time I lost track of how Saint Francis or holy Schweitzer would fare on a wilderness farm.

I'm sad that the visits of wild beings have diminished over our years here. Our human clamor and smell are established, and three dogs take their guardianship too seriously. But coyotes still creep to the woods' edge under full moonlit nights, and great hawks and eagles still glide our skyways. Because a few porcupines continue to brave our quarters in garden season, and the dogs have short memories, the rifle still hangs in its cradle over the door. We don't use it often; the conscience can bear only so much responsibility. I still dream of a resolute day when we can put it away forever. But I dream too of the peaceable kingdom which nature, if it is to flourish, can never be.

APOSTROPHE VII

Day of the Wolf

There's a flurry every so often in the Portland newspapers of reported wolf sightings. Such accounts incur the rote pooh-poohs of wildlife authorities and the skepticism of narrow-eyed naturalists. I keep my counsel, but can't help smile.

One dawn of many seasons ago, we were awaked by our dog's whining. Now Punkin is not a hound given to whimpers. Let one intruder, be it hooved, clawed, winged or two-footed, even sniff at our cabin's vicinity and she's off in a yapping commotion loud enough to stir stones. But this morning, there was no mistaking, whining she was. Still half asleep, I peered out my loft window until I spied her below, huddled close to the cabin wall. Her body seemed almost spastic. Her eyes were glued to a spot on the hill. I scanned the slope for the cause of her tremors, until my eye caught a brief movement in the gray dawning light. My breath stopped. There at the crest of the hill, hard by the duck-pond, stood a huge, silver, thick-ruffed and bushy-tailed—a shepherd dog? Coyote? My spine tingled. No, by God, that was a wolf! Staring as calmly and lordly as he had every right to, as though he made this jaunt each day. Arrogantly.

I don't know how long I lay there frozen with watching —time melds during epiphanies—but Mike was soon beside me, peering too. Before either of us could recover our senses or find our tongues, the creature turned and loped up the hill, his tail proud and high. Punkin bellied under the cabin, demeaned. I stared at the empty hillside, holding the vision.

Off and on through the growth of that day, we confirmed each other's sighting, fearful it might escape or become apparition if we dared let it go. Through the night we crept to the porch, the windows, listening for a signal of its return. The wolf had touched something in us, something too easily buried under the commonplace of routine and familiarity. To our sorrow, we never saw a sign of him again.

In the days that followed, it came to us that we dared not share this experience. If word of our rare caller were to get out, who knew what gun-happy simple might feel threatened, or worse, itch to carve a wolf notch in his stock? Finally, bursting to tell our tall tale to some friendly, we called a wise woodsman we knew, a fellow we trusted to value the visitor's right to existence. He confirmed that the beast hadn't been a mere haunt, that an occasional wolf does find its way to these parts. He agreed we'd been wise to keep still, which was sad.

Sadder still is the suspicion I nurse that we came to the wilderness none too soon to share it with wild companions. For all the protective strictures in the universe make little dent in most countrymen's ways. Unpoliced lords of their land, they feel they've every right to command its ecology. If deer forage their crops or the likes of eagles and coyotes maraud their charges, the wildlings will feel the hand of their sly revenge, and the naïve city slickers' law be damned. Living among them, we try to understand. But there's a notion which nags us that the world isn't man's oyster, that balance must ride over greed before greed consumes creaturekind.

I remember a fleeting feeling that singular morning that the wolf was watching *us*, taking our measure; scorning maybe, with a wily and haunted awareness, the greatest predator of them all, man-unkind.

Doth Not a Fly Feel?

Stone-hearted friends tell me I'm too ready to transfer human qualities to "lower" animals. In their eyes, this is a dumb thing to do, though I can't quite figure out why. Neither can the fellow-fleshed creatures.

For example, I'm sure most furred, feathered and hooved beings know loneliness. As people need people—and all but a few saints and hermits seem to—so animals thrive on the company of their kind, or at least a friendly facsimile.

Admittedly, my reckoning rests at times on a shaky foundation. Each time I hear a coyote baying at the moon, my heart sinks. Poor thing, he's misplaced his mate, I worry, or maybe his best buddy gave up the ghost in a trap, and he's supplicating the heavens for a hint of that old coyote grin. The fact that the coyote chorus occurs most regularly when the moon is at its fullest does no more to lessen my empathy than does the rise of successive howls diminish my sense of the leader's desolation.

But when it comes to domestic creatures, ah, my attributions of kinship know no bounds.

I submit as evidence Tylwyth, our elder goat. She gave issue to two billy kids recently. As dear as they were, we agreed that our farm needed billy goats like it needed a plague of locusts, so when they were five days old we sold them to a farmer down the river. It came as no surprise to me that Tylwyth was forthwith inconsolable. Over the first days of her loss, she roamed about bawling, nosing into the wood-pile for her lost babes, examining and re-examining each corner of her barn quarter. The company of her pregnant daughter proved little balm to her sorrow. By night, she bleated pitifully, and by day shorted her milk and waxed into a pensive sulk. It goes without saying that I felt like Judas incarnate. Burdened with my wrongdoing, I tried every distraction I could think of to counter her loss: extra creep with her oats, apples exhumed from the cellar, the first fresh shoots of spring comfrey. I took time from my chores on the hour to sit at her side and try to explain the reasons for our kidnapping, and point out there would be other kids in legion giving joy to her ultimate days. To no avail. She merely stared at me stubbornly and continued her search.

A month on, her daughter Sable brought forth a single lovely girl Nubian. Once we'd greeted this new blessing and ministered to her and her mother, it came to our attention that Tylwyth was no longer fussing. Instead, she lay in the nursery corner, watching the post-partum procedure, her eyes sleepy and satisfied. I could even swear the hint of a smile crossed her visage.

In the days that followed, Tyl took care not to interfere with her granddaughter's upbringing. Sable was proudly pos-sessive of her new charge and must have, I figured, warned early on something akin to "Please, Mother, let me do this myself." But the very proximity of a substitute youngster seemed to give Tylwyth a new lease on life. It's the way it is ever with grannies, I guess, once their own get has foresworn the nursery.

If I might wax philosophic, I'm sure it would do us no harm to reverse such anthropomorphism as mine and study the unprofound creatures for inkling of our own bases of joy

and yearning. Though I don't claim to know all the connections, our flesh, blood and senses aren't that far apart. To belittle their sensitivities gives short shrift to our own.

Returning to the creatures' need of companionship, I'm reminded of our drake and his mate.

Sir Francis and Merry were ducklinghood sweethearts, having become inseparable early in their upbringing. During the first year of their maturity, Merry, in late spring, betook herself to a bush in the meadow where she laid a clutch of eggs and brooded over them in proper maternal fashion. (It had taken her a while to get the gist of the matter; in earlier weeks, she had dropped eggs any place she happened to be when the urge came upon her, to the delight of our egg-hunting dogs.) Sir Francis hovered around the nest for a few days, uttering pleading honks that she come out to play, but he finally seemed to adopt the notion of parenting and let her be. With eye ever down-meadow, he appeared content to knock about the farm quarters minding his own drakish business. Then finally, over a month into Merry's seclusion, she reappeared on the hillside with thirteen balls of cheeping gold fluff in her wake. Sir Francis, at the crest of the hill, announced the event to the treetops. His clatter of greeting, and what I am sure was fatherly pride, was enough to make the boughs shudder.

There is a woeful ending to that part of the tale. Before the thirteen youngsters reached puberty, a heartless hound sneaked up from the valley and made breakfast, lunch, dinner, of the whole nursery. In truth, neither parent seemed much to mind. Maybe they were tired by then of such an array of kinder, maybe they remembered the old days of their carefree fooling around.

The following spring, Merry answered her call on schedule and returned to her nesting site. Again Sir Francis waddled about the hillside biding his time. A month went by, then forty days, forty-five. One morning I came out the back door to find Sir Francis waiting for me by the woodpile, a lorn look in his eye. So, under the new summer sun and the shadows of hawks soaring over the treetops, I marched down the hill and began a search of the meadow. It didn't take long. There under a young juniper, in a hollow of weeds, lay a clutch of egg remnants and a scatter of telltale duck feathers. With heavy heart, I looked up at the hawks sailing the silken air currents. The balance, yes . . . but, oh, poor Sir Francis, bereft.

It is hard to sit down by a duck and explain life's verities, harder even than to lecture a goat, or a child. Sir Francis put up a brave front, but I saw through to his sorrow. Then, just a week into his widower's lot, I noticed him sidling up to a rooster with a friend-making look in his eye, and a few days after that, spied him tagging a dove in the pine shade. If the rooster or dove had needed companionship too, I like to think, they might have welcomed his overtures. But the woods were full of dove croon and the coop burst its seams with hen kin. It was obviously up to me to do something about his privation.

What I did was to tell each neighbor I could collar my sorry tale. Before the month was out, the most sainted among them appeared at our yard with a boxful of quackings. The top off, there inside sat three youthful mallards. Shyly, they peered out at their new surroundings and commented to one another. Sir Francis watched them from the pear grove, his expression inscrutable. Would a proud Pekin take to mallards? Was he a one she-duck drake? Leaving the box open, I tiptoed away with a prayer for their proper communion. It wasn't more than a few chores later that I looked out my kitchen window and sighted a gallant parade. Sir Francis led, his beak held high, while the newcomers single-filed behind him, quacking up a righteous chorus. The four have been inseparable since.

I think Merry is happy for him too, in some feathery bower. As long as I attribute human qualities to kin creatures, it pleases me to include their souls, too. I mean, what sort of afterlife would it be with no bleat, quack or bird choir?

Speaking of heaven calls up Minnie, the pig. Now, there was a creature who put stock in camaraderie.

Minnie came to us as a piglet, a bonus of sorts to the purchase of her three brothers. Together, they grew up happily in their electric-fenced pen, playing such games as pigs do, getting into such mischief as pigs are wont to. But the brothers' time came, as it does to all meaty mortals, and with lumps in our throats, we hied them off to their execution. Minnie stayed home, saved by her female fortune to swell pigdom's rank.

It wasn't hard to discern that she missed her playmate kin sorely. For days after their final journey, she stood at her fence and squealed up an earsplitting storm. Every so often, I went to her side to console her, and though she basked in the attention, her raucous plaint only increased when I returned to my chores. On the third day of her solitude, she learned how to short out the fence wire. There I was, minding my garden business, when I heard a snort-snuffle at my back. Beyond the gate, Minnie stood grinning at my surprise, then backed off to run circles around the orchard in homage to her liberation. I tried to look stern, tried to shout "Shame!" at her heel-kicking behind, but it came out only a sigh. She hadn't had so much fun since she and her brothers had made a moat of the rose garden.

So I leaned on the gate and watched her antics, and once they seemed to unwind, called her back to my side. How *was* I to get her up the hill to her quarters? Two hundred pounds with no handles wasn't prone to tugs and shoves. Better go up get Mike, I supposed, and maybe together. . . . Up the hill I started, and lo, Minnie jogged at my side. A little trot here to nose up a weed clump, a little jig there for sheer joy, and back to my path for our dual stroll. All the way to the shorted-out fence of her pigyard. She didn't even seem to mind the enclosure now that she'd proven its escapability.

For our own silly security, we got the juice back in the wires. The next day, Minnie appeared in the yard, ready for play. And two days later, and then with clockwork regularity. Never at night, never when I wasn't visible at some post for a touch of companionship or a romp. I came to look forward to Minnie's escapes as much as I did to my goat-tagged woods forays and hidden-egg hunts. To live with the animals is to have such fun as lost childhood harbors, is to relearn what grown-ups disdain, the fine art of unselfconscious frolic.

I have no notion of the extent of creature communion beyond my own kind's, and I doubt anyone will shortly discover (or that many care, for that matter) how a goat, pig, or merest fly *feels* in the plumb of its being. But given the fact we share the same source and creation, I mean to continue my allegations from the viewpoint I trust best and honor. Mine.

A Bug
by Any Other Name

Bug: "Any crawling insect with sucking mouthparts and fore-wings thickened toward the base." Though that's all in the world Webster gives them, I look upon them as little brothers who, though minute, are amazingly hardy, versatile and even, often, brave.

In San Francisco it was cockroaches I got to know best. Not right away, for our polished, posh and modernized old flat (thereby defaced) wasn't at first a welcome shelter for secretive beings. But being an inveterate hanger-upper, I soon had the kitchen and bathroom walls smothered with posters, post cards, clipped recipes, menus and such other treasures as fall into a junker's hands. Each hung thing had a nice dark backside which the roaches took little time to notice. At first there were just the scouts, a few dark shiny scurriers of shelves and walls who made hasty tracks when the lights went on or a door was set ajar. It didn't take them long to bring in the troops.

"What are we going to do about these roaches?" Mike took to wailing. (Years of proselytizing hadn't yet brought him around to my open house view.)

"You could try talking to them," I'd answer. But no, the

monster instead brought in roach powder and spread it around every corner. When he was gone, I quickly swept it away.

"Poor things," I consoled the darkness. "Forgive him, he's a mere byproduct of his culture."

Next it was boric acid he brought to the battle, which someone had told him they would walk in and, cleaning their dainty paws, lick off and die of. (Who said roaches are dirty? Do you bathe your feet on the hour?) A rotten trick, I thought, mopping up the white remains. "Don't worry, bugs," I reassured them. "In me you have a friend."

Finally, against my firmest advice, Mike called the landlady, declaring that for the rent we were paying we shouldn't have to share our quarters.

"Fink!" I accused.

"Roaches!" the landlady wailed. "In *my* apartment?" She was a proud sort, and about as warm toward her fellow creatures as a cat to a mouse. I chuckled secretly, savoring a touch of revenge. She had steadily refused to let so much as a cat cross her premises. "They smell," she had countered my earlier pleas. Well, roaches didn't smell, and what's more, they took footbaths every hour.

She pinned me down on the phone a few days later. "About those bugs . . . " The very word shuddered.

"Oh, they're okay," I interjected. "Mike tends to exaggerate, I'm afraid."

"You don't have roaches?"

"Well, just a few, but they don't bother a soul. Their habits, contrary to the bad press they get, are quite neat. In fact, the biggest one—I call him Sam— " Click. The dead phone was ice in my hand.

That night, I peered into the cabinets and behind the walls' paraphenalia. "Sam and friends," I whispered, "I have given it my best and failed. Technology is about to take over, and if you know what's good for you, you'll be out of here before dawn's early light."

When the exterminators arrived the next day, white-garbed and surgeon-masked, with only their heartless eyes showing, I let them in and fled by the same door. Hours later, when I returned, the apartment smelled like a chemical factory. It was ghostly still. Tenuously, I opened the farthest cupboard door and on tiptoe, peered into its deepest corner. One lone, frazzled roach stared back. "My hero," I murmured, pushing him a crumb.

The next morning, the downstairs neighbor knocked timidly at the door. "Listen," he whispered, glancing over his shoulder, "I found some, uh, well, some roaches in my closet this morning, and I don't want the landlady to find out. Do you know anything I could do about them?"

I smiled. "Good show, Sam."

Once upon a time, we went camping in the southwestern deserts every stretch of free days we could filch. There we hailed the jack-rabbits who loped in front of our wheels, and at night welcomed the kit foxes circling our fire at a wary distance, awaiting their chance at thieving our stores. Coyotes yipped from the moonshadowed hills, and occasionally we came across a desert tortoise wallowing, slow as a century, across the continent of a sandy hollow. But best and most numerous on our journeys was the desert's insect cosmology.

There was, for instance, the circus beetle (*Eleodes armata*), a stove-black, inch-long creature who tumbled about the campsite with such fire-eyed purpose I was sure his mission was to find an honest being. When human invaders seemed to threaten, this creature displayed the courageous habit of

standing stock-still and turning his tail to the heavens, a
gesture more gracefully defiant than any human counterpart
extant. What's more, my beetle friend literally raised a
mighty stink from its nether region if its dignity was further
compromised. I couldn't but admire such effective defense,
one so expressive but wisely non-lethal.

One night, as we squatted around our desert campfire, a
locust of some sort strode forward from out of nowhere and
hurled himself directly, without so much as a faretheewell,
into the flames. Another followed, and then another. While
I tried to waylay the massing lineup with my hand, Mike
yanked a few already singed bodies from the cinders. (He's
not all bad.) But nature contains its own kismets, and it came
to us that we might be tinkering with some minute but vital
balance, so we sat back and watched the hordes descend into
the holocaust. I pondered on lemmings and human wars and
heaved a heavy sigh. Malthus might have built a theory out
of those hoppers.

Our mountain haven presents a whole new microcosm of
genus insectum for my study and lore. Barely a day passes,
except in deepest winter, that I don't hunch down to a scurrying shape and whisper a soothing, "There, there."

"Watch out for ticks," we were warned early on. Though
the doomsayer didn't intend it that way, it was a pleasant
instruction. I'd never had a chance to make a tick's acquaintance. Then one day in our apple orchard, I felt a small prick
on my thigh, and, peering down into my jeans, spied what
looked like a belegged freckle. Unscrewing the explorer
counter-clockwise, as I'd read, I offered a brief lecture on fair
is fair, and feeding off my puny flesh wasn't. My tick must
have broadcast the word among all his brethren, for I've

encountered few of his breed since. I just hope they're making a decent wage on a body with more meat than mine.

When we turned to subsistence farming, we vowed that no poisons or chemical wonders would taint our garden viands. "Organic" was our sacred byword. Though the first summer was a gardener's dream, the bug network must have simmered with the news of our lush rows, for by the following June, legions, armies, regiments were lined up at the fence's border, cleverly field camouflaged and righteously ravenous. For a while, I felt totally outnumbered, but time and the warming season healed most of the garden's wounds. Then, within the space of a torrid day, hoppers descended. The burgeoning rows turned into a many-ringed circus, replete with jumping, flexing and highwire acts on the bean tendrils. Though I sought fearfully for signs of depredation, things seemed to thrive despite their gleeful show. I was especially glad of this one day when, leaning down to yank up a weed, I came face to face with a hugging hopper couple. Their little faces were so round and fair, they smiled up at me with such trusting demeanor that I urgently wanted to share in their communion. "Here, have a leaf," I offered. But my gift was spurned, albeit politely, and the twosome untangled to hop off to a more private shade. How could they know this clumsy giant was benign?

Just when the tubers began to leaf out, the potato beetles marched into the rows. Each morning before the dew dried I found them feasting, their wallpaper backs of muted brown and gold shining in the sunlight. Hand-picking each one off with care, I admired aloud his perfection and tasteful raiment. "Sorry," I apologized to each in turn, while depositing careful fistfuls into the next-door meadow. "Maybe you could try the dandelions, which are in high regard this year." I never did convert them to the touted weeds, but neither did I add

their burden to my conscience. It became a nice sort of ritual, baggaging them across the sun-washed rows every morning. I even began to imagine they rather fancied the adventure themselves.

Forthwith, the bees and birds took turns at the plump strawberries, and grubs burrowed into what cabbages had survived earlier invasion. Bean beetles roamed the reaching rows, and a hornworm family set up housekeeping in the tomato patch. But toads fattened in the garden's shadows, establishing a comfortable equilibrium, and the ladybugs proliferated at a faster pace than their greedy victims. That our autumn harvest proved bountiful enough for the seasons' board confirmed my faith that bane is in the eye of the beholder, that bugs are illogically made red herrings at the first drop of a feckless grub.

During our first year, though honeybees hummed about in swarms, they paid us humans little mind, what with the world of blossoms and bursting grasses to forage, and we welcomed their pollinating habit. But halfway through our second summer, vast numbers of yellowjackets made our hill their home. No outdoor banquet was complete without their dive and drone. We put a jar of meat scraps in the summer kitchen, attaching to it a sign that said "Free Lunch." The free meal helped some to distract them, and a few of their less wary numbers succumbed to the glass-prisoned lunch counter.

Our human summer visitors peaked in mid-July, mostly hearty businessmen out of our city past, accompanied by shrill oohing and aahing wives. "How we *envy* your escape!" What *darling* chickens!" "This place must keep you *madly* busy!" The more wearing among them we treated to al fresco lunch or supper, while I sat and waited with a Cheshire smile. Usually, by mid-meal, the squealing started, followed shortly by a futile swatting and windmilling of arms. Oblivious, I went about my hostessing chores until the harried query spilled into the droning air. "What do you *do* about these bees?"

"Those are yellowjackets," I'd reply with equanimity. "They pack a vicious sting, has the same effect as a rattler's bite on a few." Guests fled in droves. "Good show," I'd murmur to my humming consorts. A sharp nip now and then from a bumptious sneakthief was small price to pay for their powers of dispersion.

Each winter, we are paid calls by scarabs. Theirs are friendly visitations, in a chill and lifeless world. Finding one on my nighttime pillow promises me dreams of pyramids and gondolas on the Nile. When I spy a fellow on occasion trundling across my writing table, he seems almost apologetic for his distraction. They're shy creatures, and awfully solemn, traveling always singly, slowly, as though pondering some heavy deed or fate. I do my best to cheer them, and even Mike has come to attempt brief conversations with their kind. But they scurry off to the nearest dark corner, unsolaced. Some day, I swear, I'm going to tempt one to a hopper-like smile.

The winter snows are gone now, and the nodules on the apple trees are dressed in fuzz. A company of robins held a meeting in the meadow just last week, and this morning a first fly buzzed at my windowpane. I know the moths are waking hungry from their pupae, and caterpillars are plotting under old leaves. It's heartwarming to sense such stirrings about our borders, to know we all share this niche equally. After all, the bugs were here long before our advent; to them, we're the parvenus. Yet I like to think that despite our huge intrusion, a small antenna perks, a carapace is preened a mite at my welcome whisper, "Hi, bug." If I ever end up between a rock and a hard place, I'll know where to find my friends.

To Husband a Goat:
A Moral Tale

This, the high middle of Oregon, is cattle country. Beef critters graze at every corner, moon-eyed cows vie for right of way along the winding rural roads. Though there is a smattering of family farms among the multi-acred ranches, few of them harbor a milking Bossy. Farmers hereabouts rear cattle for market, and buy their milk products in plastic cartons just like their city cousins do.

Our first few seasons of farming, high above the bovined valleys, left us hungering for something better than dried milk's chalky stuff yet cheaper than the oozy canned product. We dismissed the idea of a cow; cows tend to court bloat and scours, call for boluses and bulls, and leave messy wakes in their lumpish meanders. Besides, we didn't need that much milk for just us two. So we set our sights on goats, just two or three, maybe, to keep us in yogurt and cheeses, to enrich our homegrown fare. In theory, it sounded as simple as pie.

For six months then, we shopped about amid the jokes and banter of neighbor cattle people. We were warned how goats stank, how they'd denude our land, and that the milk wouldn't be worthy of drinking. Such badmouthing only sturdied our determination. We'd once made friends with a

proud-browed Nubian, a creature who proved better company than most of the farmer nay-sayers. Finally, in the next
county over, we found a lady who advertised GOATS FOR
SALE, sleek, healthy Nubians, no less. We'd buy two, breed
them yearly, and sell the kids back to the willing goat lady. It
seemed a dream come true, that green once upon a time.

For starters, there was the road, which locked us, during
rain, snow or thaw, into as deep an isolation as Siberian
exiles. And when we were thus landlocked, the creatures in
our care shared our enclosure. Whether they needed medical
aid, feed, or what the farmers ungallantly call servicing,
there was no way any of us could transgress, in foul weather,
the varietal muck of our surroundings. Which brings me to
our first barren season.

When we purchased our goat sisterhood, we grilled the
keeper on how we could determine when they came into heat.
"You'll know," she giggled demurely. That was that. Well,
there was no immediate concern. Matilda, the elder, had just
freshened, and her younger sister Tylwyth was a mere pre-
pubescent. When they seemed ready for breeding (surely
we'd see *some* sign) we'd simply return them to the goat lady
for confirmaton and, for a small dowry, beg her billy's services. Simple as sunshine.

The more immediate bridge to cross was to learn the me-
chanics of milking. On the first evening of our goat adoption,
I grasped my shiny new pail and whistled Dixie down the
barnyard path. Mike and a visiting friend followed in a
shadow play of moral support. Matilda, from her quarters,
gimlet-eyed our parade, a crochety dragoness in her lair. We
entered with peacemaking sounds and managed, rather
gracefully, I thought, to coax her onto her stand. I settled
beside her, my head to her flank, just as the guide books illustrated. Three tentative pull-squeezes, and lo, a puny spray of

milk froth issued forth. Right up my shirtsleeve. The audience hooted and stamped, Matilda snorted and kicked, the bucket went sailing. "OUT!" I commanded the loungers. They hang-dogged, still snickering, around the corner. Alone together, Matilda and I settled to the quiet ceremony, and took our first steps toward communication without uttering a sound.

Before many days, Mike and I came to wonder how we had enjoyed our woods walks and farm chores, even eaten properly, before the advent of our loving ladies. They tagged us on every out-of-doors venture, and when we tarried inside, they curled beside the screen door, among the company of dogs and cats, awaiting our exit. A morning not wakened by their bells' clamour was a morning not righteously begun, a homecoming not greeted by their bounding and bleating, anticlimax. There were, I confess, times when I waxed wroth over a beheaded peony Matilda had favored, days I cursed fate at the clearcutting of my precious herb plots. But the defoliation of the old apple trees' lower branches seemed merely to increase their vigor, and the disbarking of junipers only encouraged ranker growth. Besides, what forbidden fruits the goats didn't partake of outside the fenced gardens, the late summer deer families did, and we had long ago determined our preference for woods creatures over kempt landscape. There is no tended plant to compare with the sight of a goat frisking down the hillside, or a deer mother introducing her fawn in the late summer twilight. Even the frayed clothesline, the nibbled wash hung out to dry are hardly worth mention, though I do, crossly, to the goat culprits. They temper my scolds with an innocent stare, an affectionate nuzzle. I am putty to such acts of contrition.

Come autumn of that first goat-blessed year, I began watching my ladies for *signs*. "They'll switch their tails frequently," one book counseled. Fine. But our goats switched their tails at will, a sort of friendly doggish gesture. "The female in heat will try to mount other goats," another tome outlined. Big help. Matilda and Tylwyth, directly at each evening's dusk, practiced ten minutes of just such sex play with preprandial abandon. The book directions petered out in a maddening delicacy, and autumn waned without a goat misdeed.

Then one chill December morning I let the ladies out to gambol in the snow. Matilda made a beeline for the porch post and tried to tear it from its moorings. Slavering, she then headed for her sister and bumped her smartly into a tree. The dog was her next target, and before his shocked yowl was stilled, Matilda was aiming for me. Her tail a whirligig, she moaned to the skies. I dashed for the phone.

A strange voice answered. Where was my goat lady? Oh, she'd moved on to California, the stranger said, goats and all. Did the stranger know of any other Nubian stud keepers? She suggested a farmer in yet another county. I dialed his number. Yup, he sure used to have a billy, he confirmed. Pore thing died mysteriously just last week. Muttering sympathies, I hung up in a funk. Mike came in and absorbed my tale of woe. 'Oh, well,'' he said, too philosophically, ''we couldn't have gotten her out anyhow. The truck's stuck in the snow.'' I looked out the window just in time to catch Matilda ravishing my carrot-nosed snowman.

A week later, when the road was briefly, icily negotiable, the General Store proprietress told us of a woman, just a run upriver, who had a Nubian billy. We called in happy haste. True, she said, but the billy was only five months old, and puny. Could we bring our lady over anyhow, next time she came in heat, and give the relationship a bit of tea and sympathy? She guessed so, half-heartedly. No romantic, she.

Twenty-one clockwork days after her original derangement, Matilda tore out of the barn with fire in her eye. Mike tested the driveway. Good, frozen solid. We might just slither out. On went the truck canopy for shelter; into its haybedded quarters went rampaging Matilda, dragged balking by the stiff-legged inch. In too went Tylwyth, for company. The journey was hair-raising, I with my eyes glued to the cab window, minding that the lurching slip and slide over the wastes didn't crash the goats to the floor. Matilda, her eyes glued to the other side, glared back, nonplussed at this adventure on her behalf.

At the designated farm, we spied a single goat in the barnyard, a very female, very pregnant doe. The owner hailed us from the gate. Introductions. Wasn't that the limit, she declared. Her husband had slaughtered the billy just that week.

"Ornery little cuss," she muttered, "but he sure et good."

"The way of all flesh," I muttered back, stopping my ears to the caterwauling from the truck's direction.

Back home that evening, it began to snow. Hard. Matilda snorted, fussed, shorted her milk. "It is not economically feasible to keep a billy unless you have six or more does," the good books exhorted. I began to wonder at their wisdom, and ours. Was it economically feasible to keep *any* goats on an isolated mountain at the end of an unmaintained road in pure cattle country?

The snows fell through March; our road foundered, disappeared beneath their weight. Matilda showed no further indications of the mating urge, but diminished her offering to a paltry quart a day, deaf to my mea culpas. Tylwyth, the playful, the eternal kid, remained playful and kiddish, showing nary a sign of interest in her female assignment. She was, I decided, a truly feminist goat.

April, and the snows gullied to mud. One day at the postbox a neighbor remarked casually that her doctor in Mt. Vernon, two long ranges downriver, kept goats, had a stud Nubian, in fact. My heart leapt. Yes, the doctor's wife said on the phone, but he was going out of his rutting season now that the weather was warming. I pleaded desperately for this last chance, dramatizing Matilda's long plight. The doctor's wife relented. "Bring them both over," she offered, "and we'll board them for two weeks with the billy and see what happens." Canopy wrestled back onto truck, goats tugged again aboard, we flew.

The hillside farm crawled with goats. Surely our fate had turned a corner. "Just take them into the yard," the doc's lady said. "The billy's around somewhere."

We coaxed our wary brides-to-be to the redolent harem. No sooner had I closed the gate behind me than a thunder of hooves filled the air. A behemoth of a Nubian billy charged downhill toward us, hackles high, tongue a flag, his wild eyes afire. We ducked just in time. In a flash, virginally surprised Tylwyth was mounted and had. The maniac barrelled toward Matilda. Mike leaned on the fence, taking notes. "I think he'll do all right," the doctor's wife commented at our backs, in a pinnacle of understatement.

Two goat-lorn weeks later, we returned. Yes, they'd been lavishly bred, we were assured. They looked it. In fact, they looked positively flagellated and frayed. Tylwyth greeted us joyously, her bell aclamor; proud Matilda gave us one scornful glance and shied off uphill. A half-hour chase later, Mike, panting, led her back to the truck, where she slumped into its hayey floor, sullen and betrayed. We paid the stud fee, ten dollars a piece, so to speak, and hurried the goats home to be fruitful and multiply.

Rehabilitated, Matilda and Tylwyth frisked in the summer sun, welcomed the meadow's new greens. I studied their bellies daily for changes. Tylwyth seemed to grow rapidly in every direction, but Matilda, amply framed to begin with, appeared not to alter a jot. If a nagging doubt pricked my soul, I had only to call up the vision of the mad-eyed, priapic billy to know reassurance. Some weeks before kidding was due, a farmer neighbor came to call. "They're podding out nicely," she remarked, "and look, even Tylwyth's bag is swelling." I stared; she was right. Our youngster was definitely building a bosom. I began to dry off Matilda, and spent days canning her milk for the lean spell ahead. Making soundings of her belly for signs of life, I was sure I felt a fetal nudge now and then amid the normal thunders. We began talking up the virtue of goats with our kindliest, least scornful neighbors, emphasizing skyrocketing milk prices, and behold, unearthed three takers of the forthcoming kids. ("Fermin had a pet goat once, a cute little bugger" was enough to launch me into paeans for goats' holyhood.) I marked off the calendar days with growing elation. It was something like waiting for Christmas.

The two-week span when the goat kids were due came in mid-September. Grateful the weather was kindly, I filled the barn shelf with birth preparations, scrubbed its walls to hospital perfection, made beds of fresh straw in each corner. We didn't let the goats out of our sight. "Look, Matilda's panting!" I'd crow to Mike; "Hey, come watch, Tyl seems restless," Mike to me. After we'd locked them up at dusk, there were watchful trips to the barn by moon or flashlight. The sleeping loft window was kept ajar so we could listen for warning alerts.

The wait seemed interminable. On my dog-eared calendar, I counted and recounted the gestation days, thinking I might have mixed goats with elephants. Another farmer neighbor came calling, midwife to a lifetime of birthings. "I'm worried," I confided. "They should have kidded by now." She counseled patience, assuring me they looked on the verge. "Come get me if you need help," she offered. I posted her number large over the phone, and went back, somewhat revived, to biding my time.

October slumbered into November. The harvest was gathered, the alchemized trees started shedding. Our last jar of canned goat milk stood lorn on the shelf. Rain threatened, and soon we'd be isolated again for a season or more. The goats appeared fine, though a bit overweight. And kidless. And dry. I cleared the nursery shelf of its mockery, pondering nature's mysteries and the best laid plans of mice and first-time farmers.

The good spirits who watch over our spread must have reckoned we'd learned some kind of lesson, something to do with patience and counting unhatched-yet eggs. The following summer, one of the neighbors who had wanted a kid from us bought two does and a Nubian billy from a miles-away, goat-wiser county. Once the bumptious youth had done his billy business with their does, they loaned him to us for a season.

The day of his arrival lives in infamy. What wreckage Matilda had strewn in her dudgeons paled in the wake of his pillage. The paintings we'd hung in the goat barn for our ladies' acculturation were tatters in hours. In a week, the rail fence was splinters, the screen door in shreds. Not a backside was safe from his butting, and strange odors permeated our grounds. Yet we mended, patched, reconstructed, guarded our posteriors and held our noses with nary a qualm, for if there was one thing this adolescent was good at, it was proving his sybaritic bent. His energies were prodigious; not a seed went unspent. Matilda and Tylwyth tolerated his peskiness with a semblance of gentility, going about their business as usual as though he were a mere fly on the flank. Weeks went by, months waxed and waned. Billy grew a set of whiskers and added some finesse to his talents. The farmyard shambles, even the smell came to be routine. Winter loomed, yet Matilda showed no sign of her former testiness.

In December, the neighbors reclaimed the hellbent billy. Mike and I festooned the barn walls with pictures of mothers and mangers, rebuilt the rail fences, and renewed the familiar vigil. Matilda kept her counsel, hiding what secrets she cherished in her cavernous belly. By March, Tylwyth's bag showed sure signs of engorgement, and her mien took on a weighted dignity. The nursery paraphernalia went back on the shelf, and Mike and I spent our evenings poring over fetal illustrations until we knew each goat nook and cranny by heart. The goats watched our fussings with hauteur, and napped in the spring sun as though their day of reckoning were a manmade fairy tale.

On a morning in early April, Tylwyth refused her feed and chose to rest in the barn. Matilda watched her sister quietly, then nestled beside her, a duenna minding her charge. We hovered around the barnyard through the day, and that evening, wore the path thin with our tip-toeings. Finally, exhausted, we slept, the window ajar for a first warning bellow. None came. Morning light woke me . . . or was it a new sound? There! A wavering bleat, then a series of peremptory baaa's. My nightgown caught at my knees, my feet turned to clay, but I was at the barn door before I'd remembered to rub open my eyes. Tylwyth stood on the straw, nonchalant as you please; behind her, two wet kids wobbled on just unfurled legs. Matilda stared at the wall, suddenly busy with cud. My whoop could be heard to the creekshore.

Many seasons have passed since that famous birthday, seasons which matured the doelings to full-blown beauties. Moonbeam, the gentler of the pair, was adopted by our goat-keeping neighbors and has since born two babes of her own. Sable, a package of Nubian grace, became our charge when we stole her but hours after her birth from Tylwyth's side to bind her feeble forelegs. When we returned her to the nursery, her mother sniffed, harrumphed, and butted her out of the way, turning to lavish the total of her affection on sturdy Moonbeam. Very well, we reckoned, *we* would be Sable's foster parents until Tyl mended her ways. We seem to have done well. Sable, in her maturity, is a large, majestic lady, bursting with health and joie de vivre. She too is now a mother, having gifted us with Blossom just last spring. A month before Blossom's arrival, Tyl bore two males, sneaking them again into the world between our pre-dawn vigils.

I try to push thoughts of Matilda away. Concerned over her long barren state and a series of false pregnancies, we gave her to the good goat neighbors, hoping the constant presence of their rambunctious billy would turn her around. Though she did finally manage to get with child, she aborted the kids two months before term.

"Do you want her back?" the neighbors asked gently. I studied Tylwyth and her blooming daughter, both of whom would soon be ready to breed. No, I had to tell them heavily. Two young hearty females were adequate to our needs. Once the wrenching decision was made, I got distractedly busy with the creature family. But, oh, what of my haughty Matilda? That haunted the gaps between frantic activity.

Some time later, visiting the neighbor's goat farm, I scanned their barnyard quarters. No bulky, brindled body rested within the fence border. I dared not ask her fate. They are a practical people, good husbandmen. They know better than to love not wisely but too well.

But there came a new day when tranquil Tylwyth tore out of the barn with a gleam in her eye. In a trice, she mounted Sable, then made for the much-mended porch. I ran to the phone. Gosh, he was sorry, the goat neighbor said, but they'd slaughtered the billy just two days before. Ornery cuss, that one, and too hard on their pregnant ladies. For solace, I concocted a vision of Billy and Matilda romping in some brushy paradise, rampaging the phantom gateposts with abandon. But when the vision faded, I was left to ponder again the wisdom of keeping goats in cow country. Yet I knew all the while, know still, that such wisdom isn't in us, that we couldn't, once blessed, bear goatless environs.

So I begged a new stretch of patience from my impatient lady and vowed we'd find a way. Let the cow folk keep their placid, plodding creatures, their scapegrace goat japes; there's more than one brand of wisdom to this husbandry. It has to do with attachment, fulfillment and play, the prizes our rural lives thrive on, the compensations no instructive manuals graze.

"If You Have No Trouble, Buy a Goat"

What this old Persian proverb should add, if it cared about truth, is "If you have neither pleasure nor food." Oh, goats are a bit of a bother, I suppose, as is a mischievous child or your roguish Bowser. The balance is that they give, with proper care, milk which is not only healthful elixir but the ingredient of the most delectable varieties of cheese, as well as yogurt, kefir, buttermilk, and—if one cares to set oneself to its churning—butter. (What has your faithful dog done for you lately?)

Now, lest anyone think me fanatic on the capricious subject, let me spill the following beans. First, though I'm a glutton for its byproducts, I harbor a lifelong aversion to plain old mothers' milk; *any* mothers'. Furthermore, I grow plaintively weary of the two-times-a-day milking task, which hogties us to our hillside's locus more firmly than any other single, double, triple farm duty.

"Hey, we're having a party this weekend. Why don't you two come and stay over?"

"Uh-uh, sorry, we have to be here to milk the goats in the morning." (Tempting parties and festivities are never nearer than sixty miles, one way.)

"Would you join us for an outdoor barbecue? We're having some guests from the city."

"We'd love to, but, see, we have to be home by dusk to milk the goats."

"Look, Mike, the paper says there's a super auction in Redmond next weekend."

"Sounds great, but we'd never make it home in time to milk the goats."

Once, waylaid by an impromptu celebration, we got home way past dark. It was winter, the meadow snowbound, so we left the car at the roadside and hiked up to the cabin through the moonbrightened snow. Before we'd taken two steps, we heard their bawling, a piteous sound, tremulous and totally forsaken.

"We're coming, ladies," we shouted, hastening our uphill stride. The cabin reached, we found Tylwyth and Sable huddled on the front porch, wailing still. It was Wagner, at his most plaintive. The porch boards were a botch of their nervous, trampled droppings, the door was splintered where they'd butted it in desperation. While we poured apologies into their drooping ears, Mike grabbed the bucket and led them to the barn. He returned with a pittance. "They're so upset they're plugged up," he explained. "We'd better go reassure them before bedtime." Which we did, with guilt heavy on us. Ridiculous, to fret so over one's creatures, silly to let them rule you so. Until we remember a time when it was just office hours and clocks which held us in thrall.

A story was recently told us of a fellow who, when he had to forego too many parties for the sake of his goats' milking schedule, up and sold the critters post-haste. He was last seen well into his cups, probably trying to drown his goat-lorn sorrow. I sympathize, I understand. I hope his store-bought milk curdles and sweet goat teats haunt his dreams.

"How can I possibly cook and bake and look after the chickens and feed the dogs, cats, ducks, and keep the cabin shipshape and bring in the winter wood and tend the summer garden and wash and iron and milk the goats and write, *too*?" I demand, those times a deadline threatens or an editor waxes impatient at my snail's pace. Mike pins me with a LOOK. "Okay, we'll sell them and set ourselves free."

"*Sell* them! Sell sweet Tylwyth and our firstborn, Sable, and little Blossom? You monster, have you no heart?" Of course he has, and a sneakily applied psychology too.

"Then I'll milk," offered nobly. And he does, for weeks at a time, or until one morning dawns so bright and the goat bells sound so urgent that I must reclaim my chummy ritual of leaning into my ladies' soft flanks and watching the steam rise from the foaming bucket and smelling the reeky farm vapors and watching the sun dance on the hay-mucked floor while the ducks parade past blathering and the hens peck about my feet and sweet Blossom nuzzles my arm as if to say, "How good we're here together for the promise of such a day."

Freedom. I suppose the city-tied would think we had it, to the nth degree. Yet though no man or machine is our master, the barnyard ties its knot around our lives. And I know deep within me that it's not just the cheeses Mike concocts from our goats' milk, nor the sunny-yolked chickens' eggs that have become essential. It's the creatures' antics, wisdom, friendship, their very being, entwined so with ours, that enriches our days.

Of course, there is a limit. We didn't, for example, intend to be a three-goat farm. Two milking ladies we'd considered plenty, and when Tyl produced two male kids, it was almost too easy to give them up for adoption. But then came Sable's Blossom, a doeling of such beauty, her markings so exquisite and manner so bright, we reconsidered. Maybe we can sell the extra milk someday, we tell each other, and just imagine the increase of cheeses Mike can invent. Blossom all along had our number; she never for a moment puzzled over her fate.

It's a constant source of wonder to me to read of the array of troubles other goat folks have with their wards. Take birthing, for example. Once we at long last landed them mates, Tyl and Sable sailed through their pregnancies like seals through the sea, and dropped their kids as easily as loosed stones. What small problems occurred would have been preventable but for our greenness. Tyl, for instance, grew an enormous bag days before her last freshening. Our farm texts counseled not to milk unless the bag were fevered. It wasn't; we didn't. We should have. For where her udder had been a beauty and her production ample through six earlier seasons, this time the former wizened and her manufacture fell off but three months after she gave birth.

Our next mistake was to allow Blossom to nurse. While we had bottle-fed the other kids, we decided to experiment this time and allow nature to have its way. "The doe will wean her kids in due time," the books blithely advised. They knew not our goat's Jewish Mother bent nor Blossom's bottomless belly. When at four months, the glutton was still thieving her mother's yield, we tried separating the pair. That segregation lasted all of four hours. The duet of bawling dinned every hill within miles. Pathetic as it was, such racket could have been borne, but when Sable bashed her horns into the fencepost, trying to liberate her woeful child, the lesson was well taken. Some mothers would rather perish than cut the cord.

One reason we reckon our goats have freshened so successfully lies in our having let them come to full maturity before
inviting a billy to, in the Biblical sense, know them. Admittedly, such caution wasn't always taken through choice, but
once the goat-raising neighbors began importing males for
borrowing, we chose, wisely I feel, not to rush them into
hasty union. They must, we insist, reach a year at least, and
six months more offers a healthy bonus. Neither do we hold to
yearly breeding as a matter of course. When Tyl's milk production hadn't dropped appreciably over eight months, we
decided to leave her be. She returned her extra seasons of
freedom from responsibility by giving us copious quantities
all through that spring and summer. This year, with her
production waning so rapidly, she'll have no such lengthy recess. She has a blind date with the valley billy the minute
she shows signs of amour.

"Trouble," you persnickety ancient Persians? Well, maybe, if you think the sky is falling when a few trees are de-
barked for a between-meal snack (an event easily remedied
by the application of chicken wire) or if you don't appreciate
the entertainment of kids' ballet atop Volkswagen roofs and
porch-sheltered freezers, or if you don't like curious goat
noses in all your outdoor business. Or if you rear (oh, choice
term!) billies.

Until we lived cheek-by-jowl with a borrowed succession,
I couldn't imagine what folks had against the likes of Billy
Whiskers. The first we appropriated for our ladies' needs was
a cute little fellow, and too young, I reasoned, to have acquired our mature goats' dignity. But did he *have* to threaten
constantly to explode into our windows, and why *was* it such
a great source of delight to butt one from behind when one's

arms were fullest and the path slick as wax? And couldn't he
tell I was not his generic kind when the amorous spirit fell
upon him, which was almost constantly? When his owners
reclaimed him after a three-month visit, we celebrated the recapture of our wholeness and were amazed at how peaceful
a farm could be.

Maybe, we calculated, if we brought up our own billy,
gently, and with the attention we were wont to lavish on our
ladies, his character would be more exemplary. Having gotten
wind of this new plan, our goat-keeping neighbor landed on
our doorstep one day, hanging for dear life onto a gunny sack
which appeared to be in a state of frenzy.

"Got your billy," he grinned, upending the bundle. The
tiny creature lit on all fours and bounced in no time at all
onto the woodpile's topmost height. "He's an active one,"

the neighbor bragged needlessly, "and only five days old, at that." Poor baby, I thought, torn so early from his mother's side. He leapt from the woodpile onto the truckbed, his ears asail. "What a pretty silver coat," I remarked. "Off!" Mike shouted. In answer, Silver rose onto his hind quarters, pawed the air and snorted mightily. "Gently," I reminded Mike.

By the time Silver was three months old, the truckbed was a pulp, the Volkswagen had the appearance of having been through a bombardment, the outside freezers were irreparably pockmarked, and our rears were shades of puce and bile. By the time Silver was four months old, Tylwyth and Sable knew not a moment's peace. By the time Silver was six months old, both ladies were unquestionably pregnant. Which created a new dilemma, since our neighbor had acquired a billy of his own, and Silver's services were no longer in demand.

"We could slaughter him," Mike suggested one morning, rubbing his sore behind.

"Could you really do that, after we've raised him from a baby?"

"Right at this moment, I'd like to. . . ." He took a breath. "Well, maybe I could get Len to do it."

"And could you eat him then?"

"Sure, why not? Chevon's good stuff. I mean, the meat larder's pretty low, and he *has* been a pain in the ass, and. . . ." Silver bounded into sight, his bulging eyes seeking fresh mischief. Mike stared, shifting his feet. "I'll call Len," he muttered. "He's going to the Hermiston stock auction tomorrow." I nodded numbly, remembering the times I'd held the leggy tad in my lap . . . which was way before he tore the goatyard fence asunder, before he left the picnic table in shreds, and unthinkably before he bulled his way into my berry patch.

Argue about nature vs. nurture until the cows come home, when it comes to billies, those Persians said a mouthful. But one unkind word about the distaff side of goatdom, and I warn you, it's twenty paces and pistols in a sweet goat-belled dawn.

APOSTROPHE VIII

The County Fair

It's a nice little fair, homey and without pretension, much like the county it's part of. Except for the shiny rigs parked in front and the ladies' apparel, it could be straight from a set of *Our Town*.

I'd never been to a county fair before we moved here, never been because I hadn't in all my years given much mind to the sizes of onions and the secrets of prize husbandry. Home-canned goods, in my earlier days, ranked right down there with dental caries.

This year, the fair's onions looked gorgeous, and the pigs and lambs appeared prize-winners all. I suspect the drought was to blame for the relative scantiness of canned victuals, but the craftmanship of the 4-H'rs' handmades more than made up for the barren shelves where I had come to expect an array of jams and jellies and swimming vegetables to be.

It was enlightening this time to browse the displays through an outsider's vision. Mine tends to get used to, is apt to blur the familiar and fail to freshly see. The stranger in this case was a dear friend from a distant city, here on vacation with her citified, country-bent son. She hadn't been to a rural fair in all her adulthood, not since she left the hills of New England an ice age ago. Remembrance of things past crowded her expectations; she especially recalled endearingly spreads of old patchwork, and winsome clutches of pigs.

So we were off to The Fair, on a sun-beaten day, I vowing an objective perspective and the uncritical eye of a guide. First, in tandem, friend and I ooh'ed and aah'ed at the art work, the washes of weathered outbuildings and luminous, spuming seashores, the inevitable sketches of horses featured as no horse can be. The arrangements of dooryard flowers came next on our tour, the late summer's palette of cosmos, marigolds, asters. "Why don't you grow these?" friend asked, her nose in a blue-ribboned rose.

"I tried, but the goats ate them."

I ushered her quickly into the handiwork section, where she fingered the fine crocheted doilies and knitted shawls, admired the embroidered pillowslips and tatting-fringed towels with the eye of a needlework pro. When her attention was caught by a spread of prismatic patchwork, her face beamed—and fell. She sidled closer, squinting. "They're almost all damn *synthetics*," she moaned. "Whatever happened to calico and good simple cotton?"

I muttered an excuse about washability, but she was not mollified.

Her voice rose. "All that tradition, that craftsmanship, wasted on this sleazy material! It's a *crime.* . . ."

"Ssh," I said, pulling her past the ladies who were beginning to glower our way. For distraction and possibly safety, I urged my bristling guest toward the baked goods and eggs. Caught up by the country look of the counters, she gazed over the plates of fat brown eggs.

"Why aren't yours that big?" she demanded.

"Some are, sometimes, but never at fair time. My hens are very private about their wares."

"Amazing," she breathed, still staring.

"Humph," I grunted, put out. I'll show her, I promised silently, I'll find her an egg to outgross any of these . . . if the dogs don't beat me to it, or the goats play bowling green.

The agricultural building brightened both of our spirits, with its fresh, hayey smell and the bright garden provender spread out on butcher-papered tables. Together we amazed over a full moon of a squash, together wondered at the un-earthly size of the onions, the stout, flesh-colored spuds. My friend hovered over a huge crimson tomato. "It puts your small green ones to shame."

"We had a frost the fourth of July," I reminded her.

"And just look at the size of that cauliflower . . ."

"The gophers got most of mine . . ."

"And those lovely green beans . . ."

"Mine gave up the ghost when the springs petered out."

To lay balm on my fraying spirits, she bought us hot dogs at the rodeo grounds stand. Her son joined us for the treat, exclaiming breathlessly, "Hey, Mom, I saw two horses making it. Boy, you should have seen that boy horse's whang . . ."

"Let's go see the pigs," I said quickly. We munched our ketchupy way to the animal quarters. A sweet-browed bossy mooed at me soothingly. I began to feel better.

"What kind of cow is that?" friend's son asked.

"A lady."

"I mean, what breed?"

"Umm, a heifer, I think. Come on, let's go see the lambs."

"Let's see the goats first. Goats are my favorites."

"No goats. There aren't any entered."

His face was a study of disbelief. "No goats! How *come*?"

My ignorance knew no bounds. I was saved from the search for an answer by his mother's clarion from deep in a pigpen.

"Come see these beauties!" We arrived just in time to save her from toppling over the gate, beyond which a pink resident squealed warily. "But, look, they're thirsty," she groaned. "Their buckets are empty, they could *die* in this heat."

Her son frowned and considered. "Could I give them the rest of my soda?"

Quickly, I led them toward the fowl pens, where I could both calm their concern and show off my expertise. To no avail. Friend's son had but one question. "How come those hens have all their feathers and yours' backs are all bare?" In no mood by now for a plunge into sex education, I mumbled, "Mine shed," and stuck my finger into a cage. Its resident winked at my sigh.

That evening, revived over dinner, I swallowed all caution and begged my guests' views.

"Those awful synthetics, how *can* they. . . ?"

"Do your hens *really* shed?"

I guess by next year I should find out what is a heifer, and whatever happened to calico and simple cotton. I might just check out that horse, too.

Pigs Is Pigs,

But Minnie Was a Princess

Sheep, that's what we'd intended to raise. A few placid woolies to graze the meadow and then, in proper season, repay their keep with sweet flesh and yarn makings. It wasn't but two weeks into farm life before we began to wonder at this witless wisdom, for it was that early, one day, that a pack of coyotes skulked across the hillside, sniffing at this strangely smirched air. For nights after, under the summer moon, their numbers yelped and hooted from each bank and hill shade. If a constant warding off of their kind, or worse, frequent slaughter, was what we'd have to do to raise our meat crop, we'd better readjust our reckoning.

So we consulted our ever-wise neighbor. Sheep weren't easy, she confided, especially during lambing. Despite her nightly vigil, just last winter she'd lost two to neglectful mothers, and one orphan to an obstreperous eagle who had snatched it from the field in broad daylight. Eagles too? We might better build a fortress than a farm! The last straw fell when we priced the required sheep fencing. To build even a small enclosure would make the meat far dearer than the going market price. Discouraged, we returned to the helpful neighbor for further advice. She could supply us with a slaughtered calf now and then, she said, quoting a modest figure, but if we wanted to be more self-sufficient, we might do well to get ourselves pigs. They were famously easy to raise, once you'd assured the mother didn't flatten her offspring, they required simple housing, and no predator would venture near their slick, well padded hides.

Pigs? We shuddered in unison. Mike's single relationship to their kind had been when he fell into a pigpen at eight, and barely escaped with his life. The vision I called up was one of four outsized feral boars who had lived in the dump outside a vacation village, bad-tempered, vampire-toothed creatures, snorting hellfire and tearing at garbage as though practicing for something more meatily substantial.

Still, maybe our *own* pigs, raised from a tender age. . . . And Mike's being more sizeable now might give him a leg over. So we determined to survey the local pig clans and ponder. We didn't need to go far. Almost every farm down the mountain sported a gaggle of bloated porkers, gaping from fencelines and wallowing in barnyard miasmas. The idea of pig-rearing gained little in appeal. Well, we told ourselves, there was really no hurry, and we did have the option of that sacrificed calf.

But word got around, as it does always over backlot fences, that we were in the pig market. A phone call one day sealed our fate.

"Hear you're looking to get a few pigs." Yes, I said, I guessed so, sort of, gulping. The caller invited us to come by his place and take a looksee. Both his sows had farrowed that week, and he had piglets to spare.

The next day, we arrived at the pig person's barn. He pointed inside. Twenty piglets raced like greased furies through the hay, circling and squealing, while their mothers watched wearily from a sheltered corner.

"Pick what you want and we'll mark 'em for you," the farmer said. Having done some homework the previous night, we announced our decision. We'd take three males and a girl, the former for raising to slaughter, the female to breed. But what did he mean, "mark them," and how were we to go about selecting? The farmer caught Mike's eye and winked. "You could say 'tenderize,'" he explained, "And then I'll notch their ears so's you'll know your pickings." Oh, no, I breathed, the poor piglets, so young, and it sounded so painful. "*You* wanna do it?" he demanded. "That's fine, it'll save me." Mike hastened to assure him his first suggestion was perfectly fine, and climbed over the gate.

"Come on," he said over his shoulder. "Help catch. They're your pigs too."

Catch indeed. Twenty slick-fleshed piglets sped up their carousing pace; their din was earsplitting. "Here, piggy," I coaxed a flying handful of pink.

"Grab!" Mike yelled, diving into the hay. His catch streaked from his hands. Behind us, the farmer guffawed and took a seat on the gate. Our misadventure would be all over the valley tomorrow.

A bedlam of time later, our chosen four piglets milled in an enclosure while I pulled hay out of my hair with one hand and held my split jeans with the other. Mike mopped his brow, unaware his beard was a hay mow. To the victors the spoils; three males his score, and a runt, rosy female mine. I looked down at them fondly, wishing the fellows luck in their surgery, and assuring them that with a bit of patience on their part we'd get along fine. Possessorship wears rose-colored shades.

The next day, in anticipation, we measured off a 50- by 100-foot area at the top of the meadow and circled it with two strands of electric wire. In its middle went what looked like an overblown doghouse, a hand-made, boarded, slant-roofed abode built on skids for mobility. For a watering trough there was a dump-rescued steel tank, and for dinnerware, two steel washtubs welded together. The set-up looked fit for porcine royalty.

It was another month before our pigs were adult enough for adoption. When the farmer arrived and dumped the quartet from his truck, I stopped in my tracks. Those were *our* piglets, those huge, slab-sided beasts? What had he been feeding them, malts and ice cream? The farmer chuckled. "Even that runt female up and growed." As though she knew she was the topic, my pig looked up at me, grinned and batted her impressive eyelashes. The notched ear wiggled, the other flared from her head, like . . . what *did* she look like? Minnie Mouse! "She's a friendly one," the farmer said behind me, "but those barrows are ornerier than my woman in a fit." From the grouchy way they were milling about, I tended to agree.

"I thought castration made males more tractable," I said.

The farmer nudged Mike in the rib section. "How would you like it if somebody robbed your pockets?" Lucky Minnie, I thought to myself, we babymakers had something on our side.

After they'd settled in, I asked Mike what he thought we might name the fellows. "Ham, Pork Chop and Bacon," he answered, "just in case we're tempted to get sentimental."

"I don't think that will happen," I said, watching the trio upend their heavy feed tray. "But, look, that spotted one's pretty bright, he seems to be a born leader. Don't you think Buster would be a fine name?"

And it came to pass that Buster and Bacon and Ham throve and prospered under Mike's book-studied husbandry. Minnie seemed to appreciate that her destiny held better omens, and developed calm and beguiling ways. Summer came and went, with large chunks of it devoted to driving pigs back to their quarters when they shorted the wires, and repairing the moats and channels they left along their various escape routes. My plot of roses was the first to be upended, then the dam securing the duck pond. One morning I stepped off the porch and tumbled head first into the cavity they had made. By way of consolation, Mike wheelbarrowed great piles of their rich manure into my compost heap, which by then was looking pretty puny, wanting the scraps that were funneled down hungry pig gullets.

Then autumn, and the first snowfall, a good time to hang pig carcasses to ripen. Mike read and reread the stack of pamphlets which illustrated in gross detail the art of pig butchery. He shook his head and stuck the pamphlets away. Buster and Bacon and Ham began watching our comings and goings warily. They even, curse their sentient hides, displayed an improved deportment, staying docilely behind the wire day after day.

"The damned beasts have a sixth sense," Mike growled.

"Your pigs are getting pretty hefty," a visiting farmer commented. "You aiming to raise a batch of lard?"

"Umm, they're only at 200 pounds, maybe a notch over," Mike answered, looking away.

Then one day, I caught him redhanded on the phone, making some sort of arrangements which involved weights and sums. He hung up, a hangdog look on his face. "We're taking them to the slaughterhouse tomorrow," he said. "It's less expensive than I'd thought, and all we have to do is go pick up the meat, wrapped and ready, in a couple of weeks. I figure that by selling half of it, we still come out way ahead of market prices, and the time saved is worth. . . ."

I nodded. I understood. I was glad it was out of our hands. We were not psychically ready to slaughter three trusting creatures, no matter their list of sins. Now all we had to do was get the three artful dodgers into the truckbed for their final journey.

"Make a ramp and scatter grain on it," one cocky farm book said. So early the next morning, Mike banged up a sturdy ramp and dragged it behind the pickup to the pigs' quarters. The pigs took one look and beelined for their house. Instructions in hand, I carried the bucket of grain to their door and lowered it enticingly. Minnie emerged, her nose twitching. "Not you, I hissed. She nuzzled my leg. I scattered the contents along a path all the way up to the truck ramp. "Sooey, sooey," we chorused, sweetly. (That never had worked, but we favored the sibilation of it.) Five minutes, ten minutes. Buster's snout poked out of his door. He examined the grain and glanced suspiciously at his audience. Five more minutes and he hefted himself over the doorjamb and began nibbling the route, watching us the while from a corner of his wise eye. The other two followed cautiously, right up to the ramp. Stationed at each side of the truckbed's gate, we uttered pleading prayers. The three pigs stopped as one, examined the ramp, snorted, and turned tail back to their dwelling. Mike strode toward the cabin, "Going to call Larry," he grunted. "He'll know how."

He returned carrying two outsize buckets. "We lead them to the ramp, turn them around, then drop these over their heads the last minute," he explained. "In the confusion of trying to back out of the buckets, they back up the ramp."

"*Lead* them? Turn them around? How do we manage *that*?"

"With hefty sticks."

"*Hit* them? Not me."

"Gently," Mike urged. "We won't hurt them, just encourage them a little."

Hiding a puny tree limb behind me, I scattered a new path

of grain. The pigs re-emerged and retraced their journey. As they neared the ramp, we each grabbed our bucket and readied them with our sticks held high. "Swat!" Mike shouted over Ham's head. I swatted half-heartedly, and in the process, dropped my bucket on a squirming behind. Buster let out a horrendous screech and heaved himself toward my person. "Ow," I moaned, spitting dust, from the ground. He tousled my hair with his snout as if to assure me he hadn't meant to injure, but what in kingdom come was this all about? Mike pulled me up and glared at three retreating pigtails. Minnie huddled by the fence, her eyes speaking confusion.

"Pork gets less appetizing by the minute," Mike growled. "We'll have to try ropes."

Ropes, assisted by block and tackle, proved to be the solution, though one I'm loathe to recommend. It took us only one hour to get one each tied to the pigs' squirming back legs, and two more to tug, heft, haul, plead, curse, and yes, swat with sticks recalcitrant backsides up the ramp and onto the bed, by which time it was too close to dark to start for the slaughterhouse. So we furnished the truck prison quarters with hay and water, bade Minnie goodnight and trudged wearily back to the cabin, dirt encrusted, bloody and bowed. Between restless dreams through the night, I heard Minnie moaning for her fortressed brethren. Bruised and contused, I felt not a jot of compassion.

Over that winter, Mike treated himself to whole rashers of bacon each morning, claiming he'd earned them with the sweat of his brow and the black and blue of his body. I couldn't touch the stuff. One look at a sizzling strip sent a shudder down to my soul, part of which may have been born of the memory of pain. A pork chop now and then was acceptable, if I kept my mind elsewhere, and the hams were traitorously fine. But once the total of our meat portion was gone, neither of us had the whit of an appetite left for pig products. Though the kernel of reason escapes us, we suspect it might have something to do with a recall of the pig roundup, or with the last look Buster gave us as he was led to his execution chamber. I just dare anyone to tell me that pigs aren't perceptive and far too sensitive for the fates they're assigned.

It was a solace that Minnie remained, adopting me as her playmate in place of her ill-fated brothers. At times, when I went to her pen for a bolstering chat, I felt it was she who bolstered me. When winter's snows came, she liked nothing better than to chase after tossed snowballs. The tumble of snowflakes beguiled her, and she often lay in her doorway for hours watching the feathery shapes dance and fly. On the coldest of days, she crawled under the hay I took to her house each morning, until only her steaming snout showed, and the wink of a cheery eye. I often found myself wishing she had some sort of neck I could collar so I might lead her on walks with me through the woods' winterscape, share with her the wondrous filagree. Though I wasn't sure of her esthetic reaches, she did cherish participation in human activity.

As winter washed into spring, Mike began to grumble about Minnie's role and responsibilities. It was past time to breed her, to try our fortunes at marketing pig products. We consulted a local farmer about his boar. The critter had been poorly lately, the fellow said, but he'd let us know when his condition bettered. A silent month later, we ran into the farmer in town. The boar had fled this mortal coil, he told us, but we might try Fred, up the river. We went to see Fred. "Sure," he said, "bring your sow down anytime." Recalling our earlier trauma, we asked if we might instead borrow his boar for a sum and transport the creature to Minnie's side. He'd think about that, Fred said. He might still be. For that spring turned out to be one of the wettest in local history, and within a few days, the driveway was a morass, the road a gushing stream. Minnie stuck her snout out of her doorway and studied the deluge serenely. So, with less aplomb, did we.

Then suddenly it was summer, full of garden chores and a steady stream of city company. Each visitor admired Minnie, remarking on her friendliness and circumspect mien. She basked in the surplus attention, while I began to devote more time to our adopted goats, and as summer drew to a close, to plan for their winter comfort and the finding of a mate. As we looked ahead to the care of goat kids, our interest in raising piglets began to wane. Watching Minnie's food supply diminish, Mike chafed. We couldn't, he pointed out, pour feed down her forever and get nothing in return. "Nothing?" What a soulless surmise. I turned a deaf ear to such practical considerations. We'd fed a lot of two-legged friends over the year, and Minnie's company was, to my way of thinking, often the better.

One autumn evening, Mike toyed with his dinner, strangely quiet. Over the dishes, I wrenched forth the cause. He'd made a deal with Will Johnson, he confessed, to trade Minnie for a slaughter-ready lamb. My heart plunged. How could he? I knew. She was so precious to me! He knew. What would be her fate? Neither of us knew, or cared to know.

The next morning I walked slowly to Minnie's yard. She greeted me as always, stretching up her head for a scratch. I obliged, then flopped down on the outside of her fence. On the other side, she flopped down too, pleased with what promised to be an extended visit. Words would do no good, so I

tried to share my thoughts in silence, that life was often hard, and people sometimes commit acts that hurt their hearts sorely; but you see, a farm had certain rules by which it had to abide. I told her, in a choked whisper, of my abiding affection, and that I would remember her through all my days. She heaved a gutteral sigh and wallowed in the morning sunlight. We would have been happy to have stayed there like that forever, Minnie and I.

When Will's truck came up that afternoon, I kept hard to the garden, concentrating intensely on watering the broccoli, on counting each Brussels sprout nub on every stem. I stayed there, finding things to do, until dusk settled, then walked slowly up the hill, avoiding the west rise where Minnie's yard lay. Before I reached the porch, I heard from its direction, a drawn-out moan. Startled, I stopped and stared into the gloaming. Mike appeared from the porch and put his arm around me. "I know how you feel," he said gently, "but would you like to see the new arrival? I've got the lamb penned up in Minnie's yard."

The lamb. I had forgotten. But no, it would have to wait. Tonight I meant to ponder the verities of country living, of viands and friends; was bound to commemorate in quiet the folly of sharing with a farm creature one's fervent heart.

Strangelove, a Short Chapter

The relationship began under bad auspices, between the lamb and me. He'd been bartered, after all, for my Minnie, and here he was, housed on her hallowed ground, staring vacantly over his bastion, and grousing, always grousing. "Maaa." He didn't even talk like a sheep. Still, each new adoptee deserves some sort of welcome, and the poor thing couldn't know the wherefore of my truculence.

So the morning after Minnie was taken away, I approached to make his acquaintance. He neither flinched from nor welcomed me, but just stood there behind the slats Mike had put together and stared. This was no cute little woolly like those I'd seen in the County Fair 4-H stalls, their thick coats the color of cream. This lamb was lean, with wool that looked as though it had lain in a trash heap, matted and burred and unkempt grey.

"Hello." I offered him a clean chunk of hay. "Maaa." It was a thin base for colloquy. Which was all right with me, considering his numbered days. Bells clanged up the hillside, and while I sought a pleasing phrase, the goats joined my side to gape with me at this new upstart. The lamb pawed the ground with a stiff foreleg and looked away. It's Strangelove, I thought, in sheep's clothing.

Tylwyth, spying the enclosed hay, stuck her nose through

the slats. Strangelove continued his pawing, then turned grudgingly and moved away. It was then that I noticed that beside his general scruffiness, his rear end was a disaster. As if to explain, he let forth, his back to us, a sickly stream of excrement. I ran to find Mike.

"Strangelove is scouring!"

"Who?"

"Your *lamb*, he's sick. You'd better come see." Mike did, then lit for the phone.

"Will? Listen, that lamb you traded us is a mess. He's got one helluva case of scours." I couldn't hear the other end of the conversation, but I saw Mike's jaw harden. "Cut out his grain, huh? Have you any idea why he's so sick? . . . Well, if he was as healthy as you say just yesterday, his case should break medical records!" He slammed down the phone. "He says. . . ."

"I heard, cut out his grain."

"And that he was hale and hearty. . . ."

"I heard, just yesterday." Poor Minnie, and what a rotten trade was what I didn't say.

So we held back Strangelove's grain, allowing him only hay and sparse pans of water. His scouring worsened. The next day, he slumped in a corner, his eyes heavy and glazed. Poor baby, I consoled him, trying to smother a familiar empathy. Despite my sternest avowals of disinterest, it is hard to be objective in the face of creature discomfort. I began to add a dollop of vinegar to his water, reasoning that since it was good tonic for chickens and goats and people, it could surely do no harm to a sick-to-death lamb. By dark that evening, he seemed a bit perkier, but in the morning, Mike returned scowling from the lamb pen.

"He's still in bad shape," he said, sitting down heavily. "Maybe we should call a vet." But the nearest vet was fifty

miles off, and not fond of housecalls; beyond that, his services were beyond our means. I probed my head for people remedies, wishing sheep innards weren't such a mystery. Pepto Bismol? Baking soda? Chamomile tea? No, not chamomile. Comfrey, that was it! I jumped up and ran out to the fenceside patch. Good, the goats and deer had left enough for a few ample doses. Minutes later, Strangelove was gobbling up my green armfuls as though he knew his life hung on them. When he was through, I allowed him a draught of vinegar water.

He looked at me gratefully. My heart went out to him. What he probably really needed was love and attention. "You'll be fine," I told him, scratching his ear. By the next week, he was able to return to grain and hay, and a week after, began to exchange his lean and hungry look for a portrait of lamb well-being, which led me to wonder if doses of love and comfrey mightn't cure more ills than his.

The goats now visited him daily, waiting, it seemed, for a friendly sign, a snatch of conversation. Stranglove stared at them stolidy, uncurious, unenvious of their freedom and camaraderie. "Maaa," he would finally comment, stared down, then turn to a less cluttered view. The goats, their egos secure, didn't mind.

Mike was, in the meantime, busy battening up the place for winter, chopping wood, tarping machinery, securing summertime's playthings, which left Strangelove's care increasingly to me.

"Do you think I could let him out for a romp on the meadow?" I asked one day. "It doesn't seem fair, him watching the goats run free."

"Nah, he might run off. Let him be."

"But he leads such a dull life in that pen, and he's been so well behaved. . . ."

Mike looked at me straight, absorbing. "Oh-oh," he said. No more. It was Strangelove's death warrant.

I came back from the postbox the next afternoon to find a carcass hung bleeding from a tree. Mike hurried toward me, a knife gripped in his hand. "I meant to head you off," he said. "I didn't want you to see."

"It's okay," I told him. And it was, amazingly. We had given this lamb a lease of days in return for Minnie's damnation. In some sort of justice, the gutted thing hanging there wiped the slate clean.

APOSTROPHE IX

Reigning Cats and Dogs

The sole domestic we brought with our baggage to the mountain was a cat. Rosebud, an adolescent Siamese, had been smuggled into our apartment during our last harried city days, in a minor rebellion against tenant rules which had limited us to a single caged bird couple who knew not of freedom nor even bird song.

Rosey adjusted to her new environs in no time. The farm, empty of tame tenents for decades, was a cat heaven, what with rats scrabbling between cabin walls and field mice making tracks on every byway. All she required of our busy time was to be let in by dark, safe from owl missions and footed shadows. One cat was just what a farm required for rat and mouse balance and fireside purring. But no, we couldn't be satisfied.

First it was our neighbor, whose Samantha that summer bore a surplus of kittens. One of them, a muff of grey, tugged at my shoelace one day, and I was a goner. She hung on for dear life all the way home, where she was hissed at roundly by Rosey until a bypassing mouse forced detente. Shortly thereafter, we attended an auction where, among other farm essentials, a gorgeous seal point was put on the block. Mike and I gaped, nudging each other in disbelief. "Twenty-five cents," a farmer behind us called, shifting his chaw. The crowd around us guffawed and fell to joshing.

"George, whatchew want with one of them Chinee crit-ters?"

"Two-fifty," Mike bellowed. Heads snapped. "Who's *thet?*" was whispered behind us. "Plumb crazy," was mut-tered in front. We reassured Orphan Annie all the way home that she was, far from being a butt of yokel humor, priceless to us.

Three cats, then, just right for a growing farm, to keep mouse populations down, to purr in harmony by the fire.

But it happened that one day on a woods walk, I noted the blur of a movement in a high tree. "Meow," it said. I called a tentative "Kitty, Kitty." Out onto a branch sidled a furred hunk of black, its face moonshape, its mug split by a Cheshire grin. The creature looked, from its heft and hauteur, decid-edly masculine. It was, as it turned out, a sneakthief of feline virginity. Three months later, the three ladies, within a week, produced batches of kittens, Siamese and black and grada-tions between.

"Free cats to good homes," we posted in stores and P.O.'s. (Thinking it too foreign-sounding, we omitted "Chinee.") "You crazy?" the proprietors inquired. "Everybody aroun' here's got more cats than they can count, even with drown-ing 'em." They knew whereof they spoke. We got nary a nibble.

It's seven years now, and we don't even count any more. There are porch cats and house cats, barn cats and shop cats, shed cats, and one who patrols the hay rick and another with a permanent lease on the chicken feed bin. Their number waxes and wanes with the seasons, peaking in spring with new families of kittens, and diminishing in winter when owls hunger and coyotes maraud. We hardly notice the depletion, so many are there to take their place, and we view the preda-tion as a sort of exchange. Sanguinary as it might be, the owls' nighttime croon is a farm essential.

The dogs are a whole 'nother thing. There are three of them now, where we'd started with one. We didn't mean to keep so many, but most folks around here have more dogs than they need. Three dogs seem a good number, for predator protection, and to snooze around the cats by the fire.

"Whatcha grow up there?" farmers sometimes ask.

"Cats and dogs, mostly," we say. They're not awfully utilitarian, but we never want for companionship or ardent play.

One creaturekind we know better than to invest in is rabbits. The way we run things, not a cabbage patch would remain in half of the state.

Happy in Hendom

Twenty-five multicolored hens scratch and peck in the sun-light, foraging the worm bed tree shadows, bobbing among the meadow grasses. Motley, the king cock, struts the fringes of his harem while Sam, the banty, ushers his few ladies into a thicket. A peaceable kingdom. I wonder how I ever lived without them, what dawns are like without a rooster's crow, and how we stomached pale market eggs through all those early years.

Chickens were our first farm venture, the original flock adopted before we planted our first seed. When the neighbor offered twelve of her laying hens plus a rooster, we plunged right in. An eight-by-twelve foot chicken house of two-by-four rejects went up in a snap, its windows facing properly south. Four laying boxes were hung on the short wall, with a rail below for easy mounting, and straight pine branches were laddered up the long wall for roosts. We then littered the sunken earth floor with wood chips, and held open house for the first family.

On our neighbor's advice, we transported the chickens home at dusk and locked them into their quarters to give them the feel of their new shelter. Leery, I let the clucking, curious bunch out in the morning to explore their vast playground, half afraid they'd either run off to the woods forever, or head directly back down the mountain to their first home. Instead, they paraded uphill and set to pecking about the cabin grounds as though this had been home forever. I was sold. Such loyalty, such trusting adaptation would not go unrewarded. I vowed then and there to become the best chicken farmer on the mountain. (It's unnecessary to point out that we're the only farm on the mountain. My heart was in the right place.)

The next afternoon, I gathered my first treasured three eggs, then watched in wonder at nightfall when my ladies and their cocky mentor, not missing a grub on the way, headed back to their shelter. Was this what farming was like? Nothing to it!

That was seven instructive years ago, and I'm, oh, wiser now, less damp around the lobes, but I still claim that chickens are a lovely, simple collection of creatures to raise. And, even better in our beggarly lives, they are the only "stock" we've raised so far that's paid for itself with pluses. When I won second prize for my eggs at the County Fair one year, I felt I had reached some farmy zenith without even losing my breath.

Somewhere in the middle of that first summer, two hens settled firmly in their laying boxes and resolutely refused to budge. I coaxed, I peeked underneath to see if they were stuck to something, I waved goodies just out of their reach. Nothing. I consulted my neighbor. They were broody, she advised, so it was a good time to order chicks for them to set.

"Broody," what a motherly, comforting sound it had. Our order went into the mail the very next day: two dozen unsexed, mixed day-old chicks. They were the cheapest, and would enable me to add some variety to my Rhode Island Reds and to learn about other breeds.

When just a few days later the cheeping carton arrived, we

moved the protesting setters into roomier quarters, hastily
nailed wooden boxes with chicken wire doors furnished with
mayonnaise jar waterers and clumps of straw. Then warily,
my breath held, I tucked a dozen chicks each under the ersatz
mothers. At that moment, I comprehended completely what
the term "like a mother hen" signifies, for, clucking protec-
tively, each hen in turn spread her wings and fluffed her
feathers until she seemed twice her size. After the twelfth
child was admitted, only a subdued cheeping indicated the
adoptees' whereabouts.

After feeding the new families chick mash for three days,
and making sure their water wasn't spilled, I opened their
doors and urged them into the brave new world of bugs and

fellow creatures. The mother hens looked askance, scolding my presumption, but finally, cautiously, led their wind-up toylike wards into the sunlight, their eyes sharp. The first maternal lesson was how to scratch for food, and the chicks fell to it eagerly. The second was "Thou shalt not stray from my side." If one chick erred and wandered more than inches, mother set to a boisterous scolding and rushed to herd the wayward back to her huff-feathered circle. "Mother hen" indeed, and another notch in my chicken esteem.

As soon as their first small wing feathers emerged, I took the chicks off their mash and introduced them to our regular feeding regime: egg layer pellets (store-bought, sad to say, for we can't buy or grow the proper ingredients), wheat with oyster shell added, and all the food scraps not otherwise apportioned. The chicks throve and grew rapidly, and by that fall, we found ourselves with, among their number, ten rangy young cocks. Most of these turned out to be of the sex-link breed, a large, white, aggressive bunch, not famously endearing. When they began to wage hourly battles for dominion, we rescheduled our slaughter plans and got them into the pot quickly. The remaining roosters, varicolored and of undetermined heritage, we saved, staying their executions until winter, when we'd most need meat on the hoof. It was one of our better decisions, for that was the winter we were snowed in for weeks, and ready rooster proved a tasty salvation.

It was a worry to me at first how our flocks would fare through our often cruel mountain winters. When the first October temperatures dropped well below freezing, we nailed old windows over the chicken coop wire, allowing the weak sun to shine through. When November's first light snows fell, the chickens emerged from their unlocked door each morning as always and pecked at the whitened earth as though born to the Arctic. When December's infinite snows arrived and drifts buried all the familiars, the chickens peered through their windows and nagged, their plaints waxing shrewish. You'd have thought *I* had hidden their earth on a whim. By way of reassurance and condolence, I took them pans of warmed drinking water on the coldest of days, and saved every bit of green I could scrounge from our dinner table for their desserts. But outside of making them peevish, the weather, which reached 20° below at its bottom, seemed not to affect them a whit. Though the brief daylight hours cut their egg production to a fraction, I felt it best not to carp. God knows, they were touchy enough at the theft of their summer.

By that spring, what with our winter penury, we had left but two young roosters, the largest and most comely, plus Peter, our original cock. Three roosters is at least one too many, so with sad hearts and a sympathetic spirit (it *was* for their own good), we began a last minor siege. Peter went first, gallantly, then one by one, the original, now two-year-old hens. I can't divulge much about the process, other than that it involves a quick axe, for Mike performs the deadly deed up to the point where each carcass is quite anonymously defeathered. If I hear but a single, blood-curdling squawk from the guillotine quarter, I am undone for the day. But not to be totally useless, I do manage to help with the final cleaning, and stand at his side, like a good nurse, for the evisceration. *Someone* has to sympathize when he cuts open his thumb or a messy anal repository.

Early into our second summer, in an aim at self-sufficiency, I decided to try to hatch out my own chicks and forego the mail order. One of the young hens, Pinky, who hinted of some good banty blood in her veins, obliged first, producing seven bright hatchlings. In July, Blondie followed suit with five, and Pretty with a paltry but welcome three.

Then in the hot days of August, Dicey hunkered onto a

ready nest, where she sat and sat. Mid-September, she was still splayed on her straw throne, looking settled for the duration. The three mothers paraded their broods by her triumphantly. "Humph," they cackled, and "Really!" Dicey merely clucked gently, blinked and minded her business.

Finally, one early fall morning, I heard a single cheep from under her feathers. She preened a bit and looked at me proudly. Unable to find an extra chick waterer at hand, I filled a pan and stuck it and a handful of mash in her box, then ran up the hill to announce the news.

An hour later, returning for a nursery visit, I found one new grey chick floating in the water pan, dead to all worlds. Dicey's head faced the wall. If Mike hadn't appeared at that very moment, I think I might have joined my lifeless charge in suicide, I felt so hopelessly guilty. It was another lesson, indelibly impressed: Never leave a chick near open water. Mother hens, for all their care, are ill-suited lifeguards.

The following year I allowed my hens again to hatch their own. But their stars must have gotten crossed, or perhaps the chilly summer wasn't to their maternal liking, for only faithful Pinky and one bosomy buddy produced families. Oh, a few hens brooded like mad; some even nursed their eggs for an age past the required twenty-one days. And it certainly wasn't that the two roosters lacked fertilizing proclivities. But either the eggs simply refused to hatch, or a potential mother changed her nest mid-setting. Worse yet, I discovered one hen methodically pecking at the clutch she sat on until not one was left whole. For her sins, she went into the stewpot. Impatience is one thing, but I find infanticide unforgivable.

If I were farmishy practical, I would in the future refuse to leave hatchings to chance. Farmishly practical Mike nags every spring, "This year, let's send for two dozen chicks the minute two hens give a hint of brooding." "Umm," I murmur, "maybe." But below the conciliation, I determine to have a good talk with Pinky, and there's that promising banty I had to chase from the nest in February who might come through. Fickle as they may choose to be, I want to give my good hens every chance to meet nature half way.

In the years of our henkeeping, we've lost only two or three chickens to disease, and those to internal water cysts, for which there seems no known cause or remedy. Actually, we didn't lose them; they simply grew progressively puny, until Mike put them out of their listless misery. The cats cherished their cooked remains. When visitors remark on how healthy the chickens appear, and my summer egg customers rave, I thank my farm blessing stars and my years of affectionate learning. I suspect the affection part explains half of my achievement, for I'm totally convinced that you have to care about your animals' health, comfort, even happiness, to deserve their bounty. Here are a few of my lesson notes:

1. Clean quarters. Not spit and polish, for chickens, for all their endearing qualities, do have messy habits. But their food and water *must* be fresh and clean, and their quarters relatively free of flies and permeating odors. We clean the coop each spring from stem to stern: shovel out the litter (great stuff, tilled into the garden), remove the windows, wire brush the boards and roosts. We then lay down six inches of fresh stuff (wood chips work best, for their ability to stay dry and areated) and sprinkle the whole with superphosphate. Once a month, I clean the laying nests and dust their new bedding hay with superphosphate, then broadcast a bit more around the coop for good measure.

2. Wholesome food. First of all, I don't think I'd raise chickens if we hadn't a large space for them to roam in. Mine

are delighted by the orchard, meadow and pine-topped hillsides, and, after harvest, the remains of the crop garden. Though they never range out of sight, they do relish the freedom to search out the banquet of bugs and greens the earth sets out. Before the first dog joined our family, they were often pests on the porch and impolite with their droppings. But the immediate cabin environs are dogs' digs now, and many a feather flies upon their invasion.

One of my happiest discoveries was that a daily dollop of cider vinegar in the chickens' water keeps them bright-eyed and hale. Further, to save on oyster shell, I return all their broken eggshells, dried and crushed, to them whenever we've an accumulation in the warming oven's container. And since chickens must have fresh water always, it must be heated in deepest winter to keep from turning to ice. This means the toting of buckets three or four times a sub-zero day, but the chore is well worth their lively gratitude.

3. Eggs. For best keeping, they should be stored narrow end down. Dirty shells are best cleaned by rubbing lightly with sandpaper, which, unlike water, doesn't destroy their protective coating. If I've a large surplus, I rub the shells with mineral oil to seal them and store them in the cool shade of the root cellar, where they will remain fresh for six months or longer. If eggshells seem thin or crack too easily, it helps to increase the chickens' oyster shell ration. Hens who eat fresh greens daily produce deep golden yolks. A speck of blood in an egg does no harm; it usually means that the layer has been bruised slightly . . . or perhaps had a strained lay.

4. Attitude. Don't personalize your chickens by naming them or making them pets. I did and do, and Pinky, Sister, Pretty, Pearly, Silky, Snow White and Nellie Gray will die

of old age, properly mourned. It's drastically uneconomic, but friendship knows not of dollar signs. And there's always that passel of undistinguished red hens, destined through their anonymity to the sacrificial axe.

Finally, if one cannot stand chickens, and I actually know of a few such soulless drones, he should buy his eggs from a neighbor who can. Like all living things, chickens do as they're done unto. They're too often scorned, made jokes of, given a bad press. I'd like to elevate the chicken to the status of the farmer's nearly-best friend. To my thinking, a chicken-less farm is a sorry and silent place.

Be Kind to
Your Webfooted Friends

A duck pond with no ducks in it is a wasted shame, so right off, that first summer, we got some ducks to grace the hillside seep. They were Pekins, a large, snowy drake and his delicate white lady. How pastoral they looked then, sailing on their reed-fringed reflections, dipping into the mirrored shadow of the uphill juniper tree. But the pair showed little interest in reproducing, and when, despite their daily romantic antics, we found not one egg, we sent off for twelve just-hatched ducklings. Not necessarily for the increase of our larder, mind you, nor even to supplement the chickens' manufacture, but more out of a cosmetic urge. Ducks parading about make a place look so stately in return for but handfuls of grain. Merry and Sir Francis took to their fluffy foundlings responsibly, leading them in the tow of their rippled wakes, ushering them at evening into the snug duck house above the bank.

But ducklings, we found to our sorrow, are not the hardy breed chickens are, and as summer waned, their numbers ebbed with it. One by one, we began to find them belly-up in the water, their small, soggy bodies offering no clues as to what had ailed them. Worse, their foster parents didn't even seem to notice the diminishment, but paddled around the floating corpses as though they were vagrant leaves. Annoyed at such nonchalance, I rescued each tiny cadaver and buried it under a nearby tree. By autumn's entry, only four of the dozen remained, adolescents now, their gold fluff smoothed and fading.

When winter neared, I wondered, as I did of the chickens, how this family would fare. I needn't have. Its members seemed as pleased with their pond frozen over as they'd been with reedy water and hillside's green. To make up to them for their loss of a plot to grub in, I increased the ration of their relished wheat. Things went swimmingly until, one late winter day, we found a young duck carcass pierced by coyote teeth beside the pond. The five survivors huddled against their house's wall looking stunned. Mike and I were mystified. The wire fence around the pond was sound, the door to their dwelling shut tight. Mike gazed over the hillside, pondering, until his eye lit on their flat roof. "That's it!" he exploded. "The coyote used the roof to catapult over the fence!" Before dark, the ducks were moved into their new, swiftly built quarter, a small A-frame structure sporting a roof so angular an olympian squirrel would find it hard going.

The remaining five survived the winter like hardy penguins. Then, in tune with the rites of spring, Merry began producing her first eggs, large porcelain ovals left carelessly on her housing's floor. Thinking to encourage her talent, I tucked a nice mound of hay inside, only to find, the next morning, the pond's surface awash with the stuff, a pristine egg deposited on the bare planks, and the ducks paddling their way through the soggy wrack, complaining. "Okay, Merry, have it your way," I told her.

Her way wasn't what I had in mind. No egg awaited me the next day, nor the one after. A week went by. I quizzed our faithful neighbor. "She's probably dropping them right in the water," she said. "Ducks don't like to be penned up when they're laying. They need room to make their own nurseries."

That afternoon, I gave Merry her freedom. It was what she'd been waiting for. No sooner had I set the duck door ajar than she waddled out, expressed her thanks, and led her procession authoritatively down the hillside.

Each day then, for a week or so, the ducks spent probing the expanded world of their farm environs. Little escaped their attention. They paid calls in the chickens' yard, grubbed about the goat yard and barn, circled the fenced garden, pried into the tool shed and had games of tag in the herb plot, commenting the while.

One of their favored spots was under the lawn sprinkler, wherever it happened to be. "Like a duck takes to water" isn't an idle phrase; to watch a duck's shower is to see joy embodied. Such preening of feathers and craning of necks, such exultant shuddering and shimmying, such a chorus of acclaim and celebration for a thing so simple as a spray of water aimed over a summer lawn. Then, each evening at dusk, as though a knell had sounded, the flock turned from what business they were about to march back up the hill to the security of their enclosure.

During this time, I found that Merry was practicing, in a haphazard sort of way, her given role, for along the paths of my widespread chores, I'd discover every so often, the prize of a duck egg. Beneath the granary, amid the herb patch, once even atop the bagged dog food. Often I would spy the gleam of an eggshell at the same time as the heeling dog, and there would ensue a finders-keepers scramble. The dog most often won, justly; she relished the contents more than we. To my mind, it would take the most dedicated of egg fanciers to favor a fried, boiled or coddled duck egg. (It begs a firm hand even to break the things.) The first time Mike ate two for breakfast, his appetite failed him through the rest of the day, and duck eggs forever after were consigned to baked goods and well-beaten fluids.

Merry one day saw the light, and settled on the site of her hatchery. The rest of that tale is woeful history.

Some years back, with a glut of thirteen grown ducks knocking about, we decided to take one of their number's fate into our hands and have him for our Christmas feast. Mike got out his Escoffier and we invited honored friends to the banquet. The creature looked beautiful on the platter, steaming, succulent, golden . . . and sorrowfully puny. We hadn't realized, even during plucking, that so much of its plump contour was feather. Our guests gazed at the shrunken carcass and helped themselves hastily to more hors d'oeuvres. Once the carving was done, a short-lived ceremony, Mike and I ate slowly, attentively. While the others were sipping their post-prandial coffees, we were still bent reverently over our plates. It was a worthy lesson. While food is just that and no more to city people, it is to those who nurture it reward and exchange. To take it for granted, or gluttonize, is sacrilege. That duck was the first and last we ate. The meal couldn't touch our pleasure at their stately processions, their raucous chorus from the pathworn hillside.

It's six years now since we took in Sir Francis and Merry. The old drake is as hale as ever, though it might be a sign of some decline that he has lately, in an untoward tolerance,

consented to share his two mallard ladies, Wynken and Blyn-
ken, with their brother Nod. This is the more surprising since
Nod, through misfortune, got a tardy start. Shortly after
the trio was brought to us, I found him one day huddled in
a goat barn corner, looking pained. Close examination proved
his leg was badly hurt, possibly broken. (That pestiferous
dog must have chased him through the goat fence again.)
Tucking him under my arm, I marched up to the cabin, meaning to nurse him in the bathtub until he mended. But at that
ill-timed moment, Mike was himself therein, taking a lei-
surely bath. It didn't seem an apt occasion to broach the
subject, so I looked around for a likelier ward for the wounded. And lo, there before my eyes stood the greenhouse, as
sheltered and temperate and unintruded a place as one could
please. I settled Nod into a corner beneath a tomato bower,

where he quacked a few peaceful quacks, tucked his beak into his back feathers and went to sleep.

Nod found the greenhouse such a charming rm w/vu, it's a wonder he's not settled there still, preening under his daily shower, sampling greens, eating gourmet grains on schedule from my hand. While day by day his leg improved, the contents of the greenhouse went at the same rate. Carrot tops didn't take to being trampled, nor beets limped all over. The lettuce, of course, disappeared within a week, directly down the duck gullet.

Then one day, before he had put his mind to the peppers and taller tomatoes, Sir Francis and ladies strolled by, jabbering up a storm as was their wont. The patient cocked his head and hobbled to the entry. "Quack," he said, "hello there." The trio stopped dead in their tracks and stared. A chorus of quacks arose, the din akin to a boisterous family picnic. The reunited stood and chatted for minutes on end. Where've you been, what happened, we've missed you, can you come out now and play? As if to point up the invitation, the three ducks backed off and made as though to continue their stroll. Nod watched them carefully, glanced behind him at his lush apartment, hesitated—and hopped over the doorsill to join them. I noticed as the four made their way across the lawn that the three leaders slowed their pace so as not to tax Nod's mending hobble.

Mike found a pale green egg in the goat barn the other day, and Wynken is eyeing a weed clump under a pine. We're told mallards aren't as predator-prone, that their colors tend to offer camouflage. If true, I think, how lovely. Four ducks seem a scant clutch for a farm. Given such providence, one of our multicolored young beauties may yet turn out to be somebody's mother.

No, ducks are not terribly useful farm creatures to keep, unless one has an overweening appetite for duck pressed or l'orange, unless one wants to pen and fatten and treat them as meat machines. There are farms . . . and farms. Ours is poor, irregular, haphazard, and as much a source of pleasure as it is of subsistence. Utility, a helpful guide, is a crushingly dull master.

III

WHAT SHALL I LEARN
OF THE BEANS?

One Man's Meat

There they stand, velvet noses twitching, their eyes liquid, enormous. One doe turns to nuzzle her fawn, the fawn licks her ear in return. A sound from the brush startles them back to the woods' shelter. The cottontail stops, hunches small, measures the slope for its safety, his eyes enormous. It is the eyes I would remember, I'm afraid, if I were ever driven to partake of the flesh of their owners.

Mike once had to shoot one of our dogs when he found her picking off chickens and ducks for a repast. Just before he pulled the trigger, she looked at him straight on, her eyes large and puzzled. The death was quick and painless. Mike was destroyed.

We're not hunters, nor even very substantial husbandmen, when it comes to supplying the meat larder. This makes us no better, I reckon, than the fellow who tracks his quarry wisely, takes careful aim, and utilizes his game for nourishment, respectful of the exchange. I can't figure out, though, how he can look into his victim's eyes and not feel a kinship, an empathy for its being. But then neither do I know how or why early man took the first step toward flesh-eating, or who killed with club or spear the first creature and tore into its flesh to solace his gut.

I am not, I'd like to say, *yet* vegetarian. Some of my best

friends are, and a number of my children. I admire their
choice. I often consider foregoing meat, especially on those
rare occasions when Mike slaughters a surplus of roosters or
someone's bummer lamb. Brown rice and vegetables would
do just as well, I ruminate over a chop or a thigh; this creature
might still be enjoying the sun and a romp on the hillside if it
weren't for my dubious habit. So we discuss it sometimes, the
choice, and ponder a change.

It wouldn't be easy. We can't grow rice or beans in this
cold mountain clime. Some years, we can barely bring up
enough simple vegetables, given early and late and midsummer frosts. We mean one day to build an enormous greenhouse, when we can afford the material. Whether we'll then
forego meat entirely is moot, though we have drawn closer
to that ideal each year of our creature-filled days. Last year,
half a calf bought from and shared with a neighbor nourished
us well. This year, it's another neighbor's surplus lamb, and
a few redundant roosters. Though our home-grown fare is
nutritious and balanced, Mike hungers for meat on occasion,
and hypocrite that I am, I join him. Ruminating.

If there is one thing a farmer should be, it is fond of good
victuals, victuals which serve as reward for the sweat of his
brow. Farm tables are legendary for their heft, for their
mounds of meat and bowls of succulent gravies, their hum-
mocks of buttery corn and fresh greens, for pies spewing
magmas of juices, washed down with mugs of fresh milk.
Which might explain why most farmers in our ken sport
such overblown bellies and a girth that belies their labors.

Yet today's typical farm larder isn't, I've been dejected to
find, as wholesome and garden-grown as legend would have
it. This was brought home to me one day in the small village
grocery when the prop. ran clean out of packaged bread—the
pale, marshmallowy kind, whose only merit lies in the dough

pellets it makes for fish bait. The scene that took place was akin to a Third World hunger riot. If someone had mentioned the invention of the baking oven during the gnashing and wailing, he might well have been set upon with cartons of frozen pies.

A long time back, I asked the local grocer if he might stock wheat flour, or at least unbleached white. Weeks later, he managed to get me ten pounds.

"Unbleached, huh, watcha use that for?" a customer asked, eyeing the sack.

"It's great to bake bread with."

"That so? How come?"

"Well, um, you see, all the good stuff hasn't been taken out." As a newcomer, I knew better than to launch into a nutritional chalktalk.

"Well, I'll be. I guess that's what we used in the old days. Can't say it made much difference, as I remember."

Silly, to feel a pang of nostalgia for a time I'd never known. While city shelves groan under cartons of ersatz "country style" and "nature's own," big hunks of country nutrition are thrown out with the farmer's bath water in favor of lifeless, readymade food. Maybe it will take the new farmers' sturdy example to lead the old back to the ungutted, unembellished fruits of the mother soil.

Blessedly, there are exceptions. Members of one of the sturdiest, heartiest (and slimmest) families in our valley are vegetarians. Their garden is straight out of an organic fairy fable, their loaves of homemade wheat bread are fragrant hosts. Goats provide them their milk and yogurt, and herbs help keep them hale. Though in their seventies, they don't stint on their work for a minute, are, in fact, always ready to pitch in when others need a crop harvested or a field plowed. It's a puzzle whether their nutritious and balanced

habits create their fine fettle, or whether some older farm
wisdom leads them to care well for their bodies and their own
plot of earth, whose grace they nourish and are nourished by.
I do know they are a living lesson, one I'm blessed to have
near.

Their life-style is what I assumed, in my naive city years,
most farm families followed. Oh, the dreams I grew in those
days: learning old-timey recipes and home crafts, sharing
handed-down cooking secrets by redolent Home Comforts,
or amid the blather of a neighborhood quilting bee. Though
there are pockets, I'm sure, of such living legend, their inhabitants are as rare as anthropophagi in this product-mad
age.

But we country immigrants don't discourage easily, won't forfeit city trifles to turn and insult earth's bounty with gadgets and phony comestibles. On the other hand, neither do we, most of us, wear the hair shirt of pioneer ways. Each of us chooses his own means of creating a wholesome, fulfilling pattern of country days.

We betook ourselves to our mountain having shed a large chunk of city trivia. The TV? Who needed it, with woods to wander and cabin crafts to explore? Power? Well, maybe, later. Even a washing machine seemed surplus to our early farm days. It was soppy fun, for a limited time, to scrub clothes on a washboard, then boil them to a faretheewell on the 1909 Great Majestic. Baths taken in a galvanized tub by the fire were akin to foreclosed child's play. Mike, the less dream-bound of us, didn't think it such sport to hand saw every board of our building cabin while his power tools gathered dust, nor did he approach construction with greenhorn hands gustily. So it came to pass that after a year of observing the snail's pace of our accomplishment, we opted for power.

I must admit that, having knocked about without it for more than a year, electricity numbers near the top of my favorite inventions. The gas-powered garden tiller doesn't fall far behind. A child of my century, I cherish the time—a precious commodity on a two-people, 160 acreage—a few basic tools salvage. Washing by knuckle, heating rivers of water on the wood-gobbling stove, digging row upon row of our garden by hand, filling lamps, trimming wicks, making candles, stumbling through caverns of darkness on sun-paltry days left me sorely bereft of the hours Mike needed of me to help with building and getting in wood and fence mending and road repairing and the world of niggling labors an abandoned farm begs as wages for its regeneration.

After the essentials were done, after the electric poles were planted and the lines strung, after we'd plucked our guitars and pumped the wheezy old organ and sung to and read to each other aloud, and knitted and whittled and crafted our eyes sore through an infinity of country evenings, we broke all our stalwart vows in a fell swoop and bought a T.V. That instrument of mind-death we had scorned on our distracted days, that monster of empty diversion, eventually, in this theatreless, partyless, newsless and world-distant land gained our grudging reception. The first night Walter Cronkite entered our cabin, we toasted him to the humble rafters and blessed this window that opened our mountain-bound world.

We still play the wheezy old organ, still read aloud to the long winter dark. We're also back in touch electronically with that cosmos which, though we fled it, we choose to keep track of, lest it do something dreadful when our backs are turned.

Since our electrification, we've added a few other frills: the old washing machine, a junked electric cook stove for quick meals, a friend's gift stereo. (The goats are fond of Beethoven, while the dogs prefer folk.) The most blessed to my being was the plumbing Mike installed two years back. No one can know the glory and grace of a full-length bathtub who has not jackknifed into a three-foot galvanized model every Saturday night and a few in between for a round of icy and soggy spirited winter seasons. Some day of some year, we even plan to invest in a septic contraption, so that the round-tanked, oak-seated commode we bought second-hand can assume its proper function. Some day, some nebulous year. One doesn't want to rush into things without proper consideration, one must keep in mind that too many accoutrements are an insult to nature's design.

"You're spoiling it," one friend exhorted, on a tour of our new handbuilt kitchen. "It's getting way too refined."

"You still buy *coffee*?" This from a natural foods fanatic who grew sprouts and mold in his bus.

"Woudn't it be a lot cheaper to make your own wine?" a bon vivant asked, grimacing at our cheap market burgundy.

"Why do you use an electric stove when you've got that lovely Majestic?"

Well, folks, it's this way. Coffee is an award I'm attached to, at the conscious forfeit of others. Though I grow herbs for tea, I am irresponsibly fond of my bitter, unhealthy, expensive brew. While tea makes for calm renewal, a cup of steaming coffee gets me to the goat barn in the morning, hides my sleepy-eyed shame in the face of the early bird chickens. Further, I manage to find much to occupy the time saved by cooking most of our meals on our electric stove. On deep winter days when the snow tumbles outside the window or when the turncoat power falters, I fire up the Great Majestic, don my Grandmother's apron, and dive into the cast-iron cave. But though breads baked in its sanctuary have no equal, I choose to save such ceremonies for those sorts of moods that drive city people to their head doctors. Wood cookstoves are good counselors, a backup solace on the bleakest days.

As for wine, we do make our own now and then, a few bottles of dandelion or elderberry for variety, and to drink on special occasions, like a stubborn case of the binds. To put it mildly, it is awkward to imbibe homemade wine unless one is blessed with a w.c. within handy reach, which our outhouse isn't. Neither will our concoctions win any wine tasting prizes, if you count the grimace of guests as just measure.

One year, reckoning that maybe dandelion and elderberry were too exotic for city-bred tastes, we planted a raft of grape cuttings given us by a neighbor. The deer thought them so tasty, they left hardly any for the goats. Which is just as well. We find it rewardingly self-indulgent to drink the store-bought table stuff with festal meals. Self-indulgence, in balance, is good for the soul after a hard day of chores.

So I am back, full circle, to our country fare. Though a person aware of nutrition can eat wholesomely almost anywhere, cultivating a plot of his own earth makes it easier by a country mile. We find it a great security to know that we're dependent on no condition but Mother Nature's, that we could forego grocery stores entirely if we had to. An average clutch of fifteen to twenty chickens provides riches of eggs, with a surplus for guests in good season. Two milking goats offer the wherewithal for an array of healthy viands. We manage, despite our mountain weathers, to grow all our own vegetables, as well as a plentitude of apples, pears, plums, and berries. To fill out the balance, I incorporate into our diet whatever good grains suit my fancy. These, and such items as flour and honey, we elect to purchase. But if all the food markets from here to the Steppes were to go out of business tomorrow, we would make the extra effort to hand sow and harvest and grind our own grains; and though our first hives foundered awaiting a spring that never arrived, we'd try again to raise bees for the frill of their sweets. At this stage of our settlement, we value the time these added tasks would consume too dearly, choosing instead to devote our hard-won hours to woods walks and picnics, to cabin crafts and the lifelong priority of reading for the nurture of spirit.

Each season, each set of weathers, each windfall or country mischief brings to the farmer a new range of choices. If living is learning, farm life is a stern teacher. But it is also indulgent, and possesses in my view the most prized classroom of all, an ampitheater where nature gives a full, helping hand.

Seed Dreams

It wasn't a light matter that Eden was created a garden. A plot of cultivated earth, rampant with bounty, is a place akin to heaven. And though the Good Book doesn't say, I'd imagine Paradise enjoyed infinite summer. Limbo, on the other hand, must have the look of a garden at winter's end. Spring is the bright hope, dangled between the two.

After months of cabin fever and its grey symptoms, there is a physical hunger to dig one's hands into the good earth, to watch a tender sprout spiral toward the sun. The best balm for this yearning is to pile the seed catalogues on the table and pore over their pages, making a vast list of garden dreams. No matter that its extravagance will be narrowed later to a more practical dimension; winter doldrums take a large dose of dreaming to mend.

I can't help but wonder what those who buy all their seeds hastily from store counters do with this tag end of days, whether they map out their garden rows like careful explorers, experiment on paper with new arrangements, study and *play*. Because gardening, for all its serious purpose and promise, should be part play. Not a competitive game sort of thing, but one of the rare opportunities where a perfectly sane, grown-up person can unbend, shed sobriety and create his own form of magic under the conjuring sun. Wise doctors

prescribe gardening in place of tranquilizers; wise philoso-
phers plumb their deepest theories there.

Back now to the seed catalogues. There are at least twenty
(possibly forty or fifty, I mean sometime to count) seed and
plant houses that are happy to oblige one with wish books by
mail. A few years ago, I narrowed my own choices to six of
these firms, as a basis for experimentation. That number has
since been pared to four from whom I order those seeds and
plants which have won my garden's private grow-off. Yet
each year, I still succumb to the temptation to add a few packets from untried seed houses, bent always on the greener
grass over the fence. There are surprising differences, I've
found. While my neighbors in the valley might swear by so
and so's peas or these and those beans, another firm's product
prove up much better in my unique soil. Though it really

pays dividends to experiment, I've rarely come across a brand that flunked completely . . . except *any*body's peanuts. (Peanuts have a total aversion, it seems, to my soil.) And I'd truly be bored silly to plant the same thing in the same vicinity year after monotonous year. If gardening were ever to turn into chore, I'd have to dig out the rusty can opener and deaden my taste buds. But there's little chance, what with the panoply of new fruits and vegetables, and a good witch's array of herbs to choose from each blooming season.

Some lofty eon, I might, in my search, come across a seed family that matures in a month, is wilt-proof and bindweed immune, and flourishes through a whole gamut of wily weathers. Right now, though, I can't wait to try that new eggplant, and I think the southwest corner needs a feeding crop of peas, and this year I mean to try putting tinfoil around the tomatoes's feet for sun reflection . . . hey, is that a crocus I see peeking out of the weeds?

APOSTROPHE X

Another Summer Day

A summer day, the way it should always be, this honeyed wash of hours, bright dawn to gentle dusk, the sky through the day a perfect blue, the sun afire. And the moon, oh the summer night's moon, ripe and heavy and too radiant for bearing, so keen the stars and reigning planets pale.

Awake to a seep of rose on the hill crests, the pine tops creeping gold. An early bird heralds a promise of a sky of perfect blue, of air currents warm and shaped for sailing, for dipping to tree shade and bough shelter in the layered heat of still, green afternoon.

Morning slow and lazy. The goats wade the dry meadow grasses, driving grasshopper clouds into islands of weeds. The chickens seek shady places for their dust baths, the cats spread splay-legged on the porch, watching flies and bees zig-zag, too indolent for chase or cat-foolery.

Midday, and the only sound is insect hum and the slow hiss of the backyard sprinkler. The dogs retreat, tongues flagging, under the porch. A single hawk circles the woods' edge, then drifts over the hill in lazy skeins. A cow lows from the creek bank, and her call hangs like a mirage over the meadow. The porch thermometer says 90°—too hot, I guess, to make-believe work in the garden. But the sky is too blue to hide from, the narcotic earth too fragrant to ignore.

Past the gate, among the garden rows, I gloat over the plants' blinding green, pull absently at handfuls of weeds, take refuge finally in the strawberries because there is more there than just summer promise. Fat bees grumble at my in-trusion, hoppers leap from the leaves to examine this giant who invades their cupboard and shade. Down on hands and knees now, I examine each tendriled clump for ripened ber-ries, fill my fists with the hoard, and for each fistful, sit back and pop the plumpest prize onto my tongue. The trickling juice has the taste of honeyed sun, of the essence of this warm, sweet summer day. I shut my eyes and pray the hour holds forever.

Late afternoon, and the shadows re-enter, leaning east-ward now into the meadow. The chickens rise from their dust hollows and bob in a clutch through the orchard, remarking on bugs and midday dreams. The cats stretch awake and parade the porch railing, the dogs scramble from their under-world in chase of a robin too cocksure of his grassy solitude.

At the kitchen sink, watching the gold wash away out the window, I wash the fresh harvest of greens and remains of the strawberries. A wild canary lights in the pear tree and busies itself in a lattice of leaves. "Thank you," I find myself saying, to no one nearby.

The day slips, like thick liquid, into twilight. The animals are fed and bedded and wished a simple sleep, but for one rooster who was not meant to be a rooster at all, but a guardian at some ancient gate. (Is he aware of his slipshod fate, does he rue his Creator's muddle? Never mind, he is the first to sight the gift of sunrise for his singular ways.) The nighthawks glide in from nowhere to swoop and tag in the plum-colored sky. The owls take up their mourning chorus, the goats bleat at the creak of the screen door for just one more chance to play. "In summer, quite the other way, I have to go to bed by day. . . ." Poor goats, I remember. Dishes done, I sink into the hilltop hammock, the huge, webbed sag given us one ancient Christmas when I had lost all summer memories, forgotten this color, fragrance, feel, this rebirth of earth brilliance and green. (Is heaven so easily mislaid, are such days shortlived reminders? Given that promise, I could make the passage easily.)

And then the moon, breaking over the pines' topmost branches, the branches etching shadows across its swollen face. Slowly, dark shapes form on the meadow, stretch black and thick across the silver grass. The apple leaves rustle in a ticklish breeze, and the last of the day's warmth sheds from earth's flesh. With one lingering look down the hillside, I shut the door behind me and this long but brief day's grace.

Outside my bedside window, the errant rooster watches for dawn. In ragged dreams, I part the dark of night and find the treasure I can never store enough of—another summer day.

There's a Phoenix
in My Garden

I've come across some compulsively neat gardeners in my time who couldn't seem to wait to pull up their plants once they had been picked over. Spring wanes, out come the peas. Look there, that bean vine seems spindly. Let's waste it. Oh-oh, fall frosts are pending, better get rid of these remnants and till the residue under. Can't leave the garden a mess. Winter might see.

Here on our hillside, with no dependable growing season, we count each weather-hardy plant, each possible frost survivor as the ultimate grace. A messy garden we can live with. Winter provender, whether it be from a faltering squash or a revitalized pea vine, we can't live without.

Because the earth seldom dries and warms until June, because snow sometimes flurries until the very solstice, I harvest my first crop of peas in July. Then once the last pea pod is plucked, I let the vines be, to rest and be watered now and then, to get weedy even, for weeds offer welcome shade from summer sunburn. More often than not, late August justifies my laissez faire with a new bloom on the drooping vines, and by early September, a second pea crop, as tender and crisp as the first, fills the bucket.

Winter weather, whose arrival here scorns calendars, invariably catches us short. The slower-maturing corn still ripens in its husks, the winter squash looks thin-skinned and vulnerable, the pumpkins show shades of green. At the first threat of black frost, we gather the green tomatoes and stash them in the root cellar to ripen. For the rest of the rows, other than keeping coverings and the smudge barrel ready, we simply pray. Sometimes, someone hears, for I have found newly ripe corn in October on a stalk as dry as papyrus, have harvested squashes and pumpkins from vines that show no speck of life. Even an occasional tomato, overlooked in our frost-ready panic, has survived, protected by its bower of limp leaves.

Because the vagrant weather gives us little chance for a fall garden clearance, the withered vines, the papery cornstalks remain, brightened only by clusters of hardy kale and blue-blooded Brussels sprouts. The forlorn reminders don't often mock us for long, with October snows readying their blanketing business.

By late spring, the garden is a sodden wasteland. Dead leaves mingle with gooey hay, cornstalk skeletons lean into sunflower stumps. Lovely stuff to stomp down, to till under, to feed the earth with for its summer labors. And among that varietal muck hide the first surprise seedlings of the future garden, the seedlings of volunteers that amaze me ever with their early, eager growth, with the sturdiness they've seemed to extract from their winter bundling. So before Mike brings in the tiller, that cranky old sod and spine buster, I make tracks to set stakes around all my emerging wunderkind, to make sure they remain. After a few figure eights and S turns, "I can't till rows like that," he complains.

"Sure you can, look, just sort of hump around this, um, potato, I think, and stop short of that sprouting kale, and

you'd better angle off here, see, because I'm sure these sprouts are tomatoes.''

"They're *weed*s." Sometimes he's right, but it doesn't pay to take chances. I'd hate to be the first to discourage a struggling phoenix.

So by midsummer, my rows are a good gardenkeeper's nightmare. Orphans of last year's tomatoes spread into the corn, second-hand peas climb the bean vines, radishes and dill intrude on the onions, forgotten potatoes nudge the heading lettuce. Companionate planting it isn't, but the companionable plants do just fine. And the born-again vegetables round out a larder grateful for any dividend it can gain.

A Most Literary Mulch

Like most organic fanatics, I'll use any stuff remotely feasible for garden mulch: sawdust, dust dust, scraps of scrounged black plastic and torn roofing, pine duff, scrambled leaves, the sweepings of Mike's haircuts, rug remnants. With esthetics lost in the heaps, by mid-season my rows are a motley assortment of all of the above. But two years back, they began to resemble less some ragamuffin's scrapheap than a library torn by a tornado. For that was the year I experimented with reading matter mulch.

Living fifty miles from the nearest newsstand, we don't have what could be called ready access to magazines and papers. But in pity for our isolated state, friends flood us every now and then with their discarded journals. While the most flammable go, upon reading, into the woodstove bin, the thick remainder now and forever more gets stashed with the garden paraphenalia. My vegetables are not only the healthier for it, but better read.

This came to pass when I got weary of spreading tons of cast-off hay, day after day, on every 125 to 85 foot of the garden, when no sooner would I have the northeast quarter covered than weeds would poke through the settled southwest piles. "Please, more hay!" I'd shout uphill to Mike, and he would drop his labors to mount the truck to drive miles into the valley to scrounge whatever neighbor's ancient mow he could uncover. Straw bedding from the goat barn was used up early on, and what sawdust I had swept into boxes and mixed with bonemeal never went very far. The woods' floor adjacent to the garden was picked so clean of pine needles, I feared I'd soon upset the bosky ecology. And still the infernal weeds protruded.

One day, after five hot hours of rooting up the worst of the invaders, I happened to trip over my stacked boxes of magazines in the woodshed corner. Like a hint of Heaven, light dawned on me. In a trice, I had the whole slippery edifice toted to the garden.

The thickest I layered first around the bean seedlings, the thinner got tucked around the broccoli and cauliflower's feet.

(I plotted that by the time a determined weed nosed through there, the leaves' shade would offer added discouragement.) The lighest, flyers mostly, and government freebies, circled the lettuce, to suit its shorter term. Tomatoes, peppers, corn, which needed every speck of soil warmth they could absorb, I left doomed to illiteracy. My final step was to wet the whole spread to a sodden mass, to prevent the pages from being prone to breezes.

Some two months on, we began to harvest the best broccoli and cauliflower crop in our garden's history from its weed-free (well, relatively, though a few did find their way between the phrases), moist and bookish soil. The lettuce, too, was amazing, and the beans did as best they could, having been retarded by a late June frost. When a boon of late hot summer days fattened my tomatoes with dispatch, their suddenly heavy vines drooped groundward, the fruit running amok on the paths. But fortune had it that by this time, my magazine boxes were again overflowing, so it was into the garden with new volumes, there to slip one under each grounded tomato. No rot nor worm would venture that slick moat. As the tomatoes spread and ripened across the pages, I blessed my literate friends.

Mike, the tiller, has a somewhat different view. The paper, rotted to shreds by the next garden season, gets stuck in the tines, he says. A small matter, I tell him; dead weeds get stuck worse. I have, though, bent a little. I no longer plant thick catalogues among the rows.

Riddle: What's black and white and green all over?

A. Aw, come on, you know.

When the Frost
Is on the Punkin in July

At first we had our farm figured as being in the comfortable land of zone three . . . "Set out seedlings in May,
expect first frost by Sept. 30." When our first garden was
blackened on September 11th, we revised our mapping—
"Damn, that must not include the higher elevations,"—and
replotted the garden's scenario.

During the second spring, Mike built a cozy cold frame
against the cabin's south wall. Into it went a crowded assortment of tomatoes, peppers, eggplant, brassicas, lettuce, and
the marigolds with which to surround them when they were
set out. Everything got along fine until one late April 20°
night zapped the lush seedlings, right through the blankets
we piled on the panes. With large applications of encourage-
ment and careful tending, many of the wounded plants eventually revived, to be set into their garden beds the first week
in June. The second week in June, the temperature again
took a nosedive, and the twice-attacked seedlings breathed
their last. What *was* this, zone two, one and a half?

The following year (keep track, now), the whole of June
being balmy, the seedlings nearly burst their bounds. By July,
the garden was a jungle, and in August, oh historied month,

we picked our first ears of corn. (The catalogues *didn't* lie.) Even the melons I plant every year in the spirit of Pollyanna began to plump out. "Let's invite everyone up from the city to an Equinox harvest party," I suggested to Mike.

"Let's wait," said Mike, the accursed skeptic. And sure enough, toward the dawn of one September morning, I was awakened by Mike's fumbling for more covers. "Freezing," he murmured. "*Freezing!*" He bounded from bed and stared at the window thermometer. 32°. Before I could mumble Jack Frost, he was down the hill and into the garden, where his first act was to grab each ready box and basket and cover the tomatoes. His second was to turn on the rainbird over the leggy corn rows. That took care of one-quarter of the poten-

tial victims. Then, staring desperately about in the dawn's
first cold light, he espied our weed trash barrel. This he
hefted, like a man bedeviled, into the south quarter's center,
lit its contents with a match, and fed the smouldering contents straw mulch pulled up from the rows. We knew the
smudge was effective when, fifteen minutes later, the fire
patrol plane droned over our meadow.

The following two years brought frosts on June 25th and
26th respectively. With their advent, Mike rigged a thermostat outside our loft window which, when the temperature
dropped to 35°, switched on both the bedside lamps and the
radio. A clever invention, but one which caused many a
sleepless night while we stared into the chilly darkness,
breaths held, waiting for the sight and sound of alarums
without. Come July, we unhooked the thing to catch up on
our r.e.m.'s. And it was in July, the fourth, to be exact, that
frost again crept into the garden.

"It's cold," I'd said that evening, eyeing the Ashley.

"Mm, a little chilly," Mike agreed. (He has the constitution of a salamander.)

"Maybe we should plug in the thermostat," I said toward
bedtime.

"Nahh," he answered sleepily. "Who ever heard of a frost
in July?" Whoever indeed? But as fate would have it, it
didn't really matter, for that was the year of the drought,
and the remaining vegetables perished of thirst under August's searing procession of skies.

Bloody mad but unbowed, I have sent this year's seed or-
ders on their way. I'm itching to try that new Canadian tomato, and those drought-resistant beans, and maybe this year,
the melons will hang on in the sheltered north quarter. . . .

In the land of hope, there is never any winter. If someone
would point the way, I'd pack my bags.

Apostrophe XI

A Strange Season

As summers go . . . and how quickly they do, the days of gold and warm texture . . . the past one was less than stellar. I utter this in a whisper, glancing over my shoulder. A summer person, I am loathe to complain about one jot of my season's scars. Still, as I say, less than stellar.

It started off well enough, tardy as always, or at least it seems always that way after stone-cold winter's wait and a spring that gets scared off by each downmountain bluster. But once it got here, around mid-June, as I remember, it was worth the long wait. Seeds came to life under its spill, hawks swooped in from the hilltops as though scattered from some cavernous cannon. The robins grew bold and obstreperous, while the chickadees shied off to a quieter quarter to await, like Chinese miners, the bigger birds' scraps. Oh, it was full of such promise, as newfledged summers ever are.

But by late June, its schedule seemed cockeyed, off balance. No thunderstorms roared with their rains up the valley to drench thirsty fields and parched forest land. Then July, and the earth thirsted still. My garden gaped at the cloudless sky; I gaped at my garden. I'd leave that smaller plot be and just water the big one, I figured, it's got more promising greens. But before I could act, the black hand of frost stole in overnight, laying low a whole sward of limp rows. Two weeks and trickles less of spring water later, what remained of even the big plot had to be left to fend, waterless, for itself. When there were a few drops to spare, they were parceled out to the strawberries. To no avail. That patch too shriveled, and when I had to give it up entirely, I felt I'd turned my back on a bounteous friend.

By August, the garden seemed hopeless. What leaves the drought-mad grasshoppers hadn't already gobbled, the panting porcupines claimed for their own. Onion tops disappeared overnight, and where kale and lettuce had flourished, leafless stubs decayed on the ground. Determined to reap some reward for my earlier labors, I crawled through the wrack and grasshopper armies each day, stealing a few peas here, a pocketful of zucchini there. (Zucchini, I've a suspicion, could prosper in Hades.)

Then the longest heat wave on record settled in. Watching the skies, sniffing the air from waking 'til sleep for the sign, the smell, the haunt of dreaded fire became ritual. Watching the thunderheads move over the mountains, the lightning tines strike into dense thickets of trees. Listening to the Forest Service band on the radio hour on hour, praying they contained that fire and the next and the one after that. One afternoon we watched a bolt strike a hillside two ridges away, lash into a cluster of pines directly above a neighbor's dwelling. A few counted breaths later, smoke plumed into the sky. Mike got on the phone. Yes, please come, the neighbor said, it looked bad. After Mike sped down the meadow, friends and I watched the bombers dive over, dropping their blood-colored stuff, watched the smoke rise again and again. It was out by nightfall, and Mike returned weary and splashed with red. We kept watching, measuring the wind shifts, sniffing. Haunted.

Down from the higher mountains then came the woods creatures, in search of green food and water. Deer families, their watchful bucks guarding, traipsed though our pines and to the meadow's dog-patrolled fringes. I pulled ripening apples from trees so the deer could sneak in at night for a feast, left hay scattered outside the goat yard to reward their guests. (And the goats stared wide-eyed through the darkness at these goat-like callers, and the deer stared back, wary of fences and apples so freely at hand.) By mid-August the porcupines were emboldened to roam the hillside in broad daylight. One met his end by Mike's hand in the woodpile, another just outside the back door. Two small balls of quills and bumptiousness we caught and took off to a distant mountain, two varmints too young and lost-looking to kill. (Such small things need a chance to grow up and choose between good and evil, between a few trees among many, and, say, my garden rows.)

One creature we could not find in us to welcome was the rattler. Before August was out, a passer-by killed two in our driveway, and a few days later, a visiting child almost stumbled over a third but a few yards from our porch. (His parents were packed for a hasty retreat by nightfall.) We'd never encountered rattlers so nearby before, never thought to tread carefully, as we do in the lower regions, in those den-ish places we know they favor.

A strange summer. All the stops pulled by the minions of weather, with a play of the forces the wisest of men haven't been able to put a fix on or plumb. But when its last days retreated and the nights grew long, I remembered it as I remember all summers, as the playground of angels. Never mind my ungodly garden, the spectre of fire, the fret over the dwindling waters. Imperfect and fickle, it was a season I committed to memory as a touchstone of generous days.

Like pain, we forget flaws quickly; beauty stands.

Where the Wild Thyme Blows

It's an article of faith that much of our attitude toward the world's things is born of the names we call them by. Take "weeds," for example. Lives there a man with soul so dead he hasn't savored a mess of steamed young dandelion greens after a hungry winter, or who fails to delight in an autumn meadow burnished with islands of goldenrod? Yet either plant, and a legion more, is cursed roundly if it so much as nudges our fussy cultivation. "Weeds" is seldom uttered kindly, nor is their eradication listed among gardening's pleasures.

Maybe we should start all over, find nicer words for the scape-grace plants. Because they're really not all bad. Some, especially the deeper-rooted varieties, can even be vegetables' helpmeets, bringing nutriment up from the subsoil to their classier neighbors, while others help break up hardpan and maintain a plot's moisture balance. And in a rare case of justice, soil science informs us that the healthier the vegetable, the less likely weeds are to compete with it once it's established. (Tell *that* to your lush burdock come summer).

Though there have been times when I have railed bloodthirstily at my garden's rampant beggars, I've also been grateful to them on occasion. Like the spell two years ago when I decided to grow a small patch of celery. I had started the seedlings in shaded flats, but when they were ready to transplant into the garden, the summer temperature soared. Fearing for their delicate constitutions, I looked about for a spot of partial shade not already promised my mid-season lettuce. Aha, the weed patch by the west fence, left there to flourish by my bone-weary tiller. I cleared enough space for the small seedlings, and bedded them in the moist, crumbly weed shade. That the celery crop proved fantastic stirred in me a suspicion that the weeds helped it in more mysterious ways than just the provision of shade.

Admittedly, plants must be given a proper chance in their stripling days. No seedling has a holler in hell smack up against a towering pigweed or a tangle of serpentine vines. But the weeding chore isn't wholly unwelcome when summer's still new and the garden rows redolent with earth smell. Come late July and the dog days of August, though, and pulling weeds ranks, among preferences, after cleaning the stables. This is the time of the season when I bless my sturdy rows, misplace the hoe, and leave the rest pretty much up to Mother Nature. Oh, I might deign to pull the worst of the thistle from the strawberry patch while I'm berrying; not all of it, though, for the biggest, juiciest berries snuggle near it for protection. And if the lamb's-quarters crowd the root crops too badly, I yank out the bushiest miscreants. But by this time, the vegetable leaves overshadow the sneakiest interlopers, while the more determined thrive at least no better or faster than the select, and the bug-hungry toads are grateful for the rank shade.

A gardening friend, a dyed-in-the-wool plant fanatic, visited late one summer. He'd scarcely dismounted from his car when he demanded a tour of the rows. His initial reaction was a gasp of disbelief. "My God," he breathed heavily, "don't you ever *weed*?"

I looked at him hard. "Please observe the health of the plants." It was no use. He couldn't see the trees for the interloping forest. That evening, I served him a platter of fresh corn, crisp green beans, and a salad mixed with all manner of greens, including the disdained weeds. It was hard not to smirk at his gourmandizing, but I did have the decency to say not a defensive word.

Every September sponsors a contest between my vegetable stragglers and the first killer frost. Though the frost is usually victor, I've discovered that those late bloomers which are surrounded by weeds are the last to be nipped in their buds. The more lush their weed neighbors, the more protection they seem to enjoy.

Cosmetically, my late garden may look like a thicket gone wild. Man doth not live by cosmetics alone, and a full winter larder has little to do with the summer slavery demanded by spic and span rows. Besides, I'd much rather look down my mid-winter hillside and see ice-fingered branches and snow-flowered stalks than a plot unreminiscent of summertime's alms.

All Creatures

Great and Small,

But Not in My Garden

I thank my saints by the season that the four-footed creatures my garden displaced haven't retaliated in force.
After all, its 12,000 square feet of choice meadow was, before I came along with my hoe and gaseous tiller, a playground, shelter and crosslot to many inhabitants. Yet despite
our trespass, and the barricade of a nine-foot deer fence,
vengeance isn't in them. Maybe they've grown so resignedly
used to man's greed by now that they haven't the heart left
for rancor.

Nevertheless, to be safer than sorry, I make it a habit to
plant each year a bit more than we need. An extra row of lettuce here, a spare plot of parsley there, to show I'm willing to
share. Within reason.

The second year I furnished my plots, I noticed, in no time
at all, a few mounds of fresh dirt lying hard by the carrots.
"Gophers!" a visitor warned. "You'd better gas 'em fast."

Visions of baby gophers gasping their last appeared on call
before me. No, I'd wait a decent interval and see how far
they'd go with their digging. A few carrots disappeared,

then some beets, not enough to make a dent in the larder. It was when they sidled up to my precious strawberry patch that I drew the line. Gopher bombs went into their foxholes, raising a stink enough to drive *me* out, but, like jungle guerrillas, the gophers seemed only to deepen their caves. Then one morning a stone-dead number of their species littered the garden path. Cookie, our prodigal cat, licked her whiskers nearby. "Good hunting," I praised her, with half-hearted conviction. "But please leave the birds and toads be."

The following year, Cookie moved cat and kaboodle into the garden before the decline of spring. There she set up a school of gopher decimation, with recesses few and far between. Day upon day I watched her sneak flat-bellied among

the rows, her young gaggle tagging behind. In the instruction of follow the leader, my rows were secure. I admit I felt a weak sister, letting her do my dirty work for me, but it at least approached a more natural balance, her feeding her own gopher prey.

For some reason beyond me, no rabbit seems ever to have sniffed at my garden's board. I know they hole up nearby, for we trace their busy tracks in the winter snows, and their spoor dots our every woods hollow. Maybe, they've enough provender in the wild plants that abound, or perhaps, timid beings that they are, they're kept at bay by the loud-mouthed dogs. Raccoons are only slightly pushier, and the one who rampaged our grounds some time back was too intent on our chickens to stop for a vegetable appetizer. (Though I don't advise keeping chickens as bait, the flock did, at least, distract him.) When I read of coons destroying a corn patch in one night, I can't help but wonder what the farm dog was about during the feast, and what a good dog's hired on for if not to police one's victuals. If a gardener chooses to remain dogless, he should at least plan to station himself by the rows as an avenging angel, particularly on those warm-mooned summer nights when all manner of creatures stalk their just desserts.

But wait; the above is half bravado. Each area has its bête noire—some one prevailing presence that tips the farm's scales. I doubt any creature could be beter noirer than our crafty and populous porcupines. Though I've mentioned elsewhere the rows of cauliflower and broccoli which fell to their predation, and the stands of Brussels sprouts that disappeared in one dawn, I failed to add that for dessert they favor strawberry leaves, selecting the most choice by stampeding the whole patch to smithereens. Other fruit leaves tickle their palates too: young peach, apple and plum, whatever is green, tender, hopeful. Their nocturnal habits would sorely tempt a saint to churl. Further, there seemed no way to outwit the prickly invaders. Fenceposts became their ladders, dog snouts their dart boards. A scatter of blood meal around the rows, which puts off the weaker-spirited, merely whets their appetites.

Two years ago, we finally came up with a solution of sorts, one not as easy as the ready rifle, but effective and far more humane. We built two eight-by-eight foot A-frames out of two-by-fours, covered them with sturdy chicken wire, leaving one hinged gate at either end for access and egress. (Human, not porcupine. The gates were firmly held shut with crossboards set into slots.) Under these protective structures, I planted the porcupines' favorite fare. Lo and behold, not a cauliflower was touched henceforth, and the broccoli and its kin bloomed unmolested. Inadvertently, the frames proved a boon in yet another department. On the hottest days—those swelterers that bolt a plant in a wink—I lay slats or burlap bags atop the wire to shade the plants. This accommodation works so famously that we plan to add more A-frames in the coming days, both for varmint defense and heat protection. The only chink in the structures' armor is that they do nothing to discourage the heirs of our original gophers. Cookie, the huntress, died of a mysterious malady two years back (a glut of gophers perhaps), and her kin never got the hang of her prodigious talents. The only thing they've learned to hold at bay is an occasional butterfly well into its dotage.

So it is back to the sulphurous bombs and parlous visions of gassed junior gophers. Though I'd rather spend my time and funds supporting the planet's endangered species instead of trying to increase their number, if I let down my guard completely, my plants may be the first to fall to extinction. Extinct I don't want the gophers to be, but, well, maybe a touch less fecund and overfed?

Comfort Me With Apples

An incurable romantic, I've always cherished stories about old men who plant apple trees they'll not live to see bear. Now the proud possessor of a venerable apple orchard, I honor them beyond my earlier bitter-sweet notions.

No one in these parts remembers when our twenty-five trees were planted, much less what early homesteader might have set them out. Few even recognize the half dozen or so varieties. They don't make them like that any more. From the scant history of this place we've uncovered, we know they have some three score plus ten in their sinew. That's hard to believe, come September, October, when gold and green and rosy and russet fruit weight every bough, when we bring bushel basket upon basket into the root cellar, and then invite the neighbors to pick the remains, and still have enough on the boughs for deer and winter birds' feasts.

When it comes to our orchard's nurture, we disobey all the rules, or, more accurately, don't apply any. The first year, we were too busy to pay much mind to the trees.

"This article says we should prune them heavily," I'd point out to Mike.

"Yeah, but this week we've got to get that roof on."

"Some fellow in the Merc told me we should feed their roots at the dripline. What's a dripline?"

"It's like a dewline, I suppose. Hey, would you give me a hand with the chicken fence this afternoon?"

And from a neighbor, "You won't get much from those trees. Full of codling moths. You gotta spray."

"Mm-hmm. Say, could you help lift this beam while you're here?"

So the trees remained neglected, as they had for long decades before we came along. And when, after the garden rows were picked clean and first frosts had tinged the night air and the afternoon shadows had stretched longer and pooled deeper, we got around to the slighted old orchard, there was nothing left to do but harvest its riches.

Poems have been written about apple picking, but for me, few of them touch the feel of its ceremony, which is altogether the most edifying and beatific and inviting of play one could know. The stippled sun through the leaves, the scampering after dropped fruit before it rolls out of sight (it's always the prize that unhinges and falls and bruises), the rough hug of the bark when you shinny up into the spread to capture the topmost beauties (it's always the prizes that stay just out of reach), the taste of the first bite.

"Here, take a bite out of this one, just *taste* that juice. . . ."

"No, you *have* to sample this one first. These rosy ones are the best yet. . . ."

"Mm-*hmm*, and these green ones will make super pies. . . ."

"These small golden kind are right out of my childhood!"

"Oh, look, get that one, see way up there? Now *that's* the original apple."

"Oh-oh, it's got worm holes in it. What a shame."

Worm holes or not, we plucked, that first year, every apple within climbing reach. I mean *every* blessed apple, because we'd never had an apple orchard before, because I'd

never climbed an apple tree. It was only when we carried the basketsful up the hill and lined them up on the porch that I wondered where we would store them all.

"Why didn't we finish the root cellar?" I groaned.

"We had a few other things to do, remember?"

"But what'll we *do* with them?"

Mike's eyes lit. "Leave that to me."

Just before dark, he called me out to the hillside. There on the one level spot stood a small block-shaped abode built of baled hay. "There's your root cellar," Mike bragged. I stared and walked around it until I came upon an opening between the stacked bales, then, on hands and knees, crawled inside. It was cool and quite roomy and pungent with hay.

"Lovely," I said. "Tell you what, we'll put the apples in the sleeping loft, and I'll sleep here."

But the best laid plans being what they are, our makeshift

cellar's days were numbered, for before the month was out, the deer moseyed onto the hay-built sanctuary and, not satisfied with eating its walls to the ground, helped themselves to its contents too.

The following spring, we finished the real root cellar, and then, heeding experts' advice, treated each apple limb to miscible oil spray. That autumn, the apples were rife with worms. A year later, we hung molasses jar traps under each tree, and Eureka!, hardly a wormhole blemished that year's crop. Year III, we both refilled the trap jars and descaled the wormiest trees; there wasn't an apple in that harvest without a worm scar. Either we weren't cut out to be orchardists, or Mother Nature was playing tricks with our well-meaning naïvete. Impatient with such arbitrary habits, we finally concluded that if those dear trees had flourished without our fussing for, lo, all those years, they might do just as well with continued doses of benign neglect. It turned out to be one of our wiser reckonings. Other than a bit of pruning here and there, now and then—I mean, beside what the goats accomplish, and beside when Mike needs a mess of apple wood for his cheese smoking—the only attention the trees have gotten lately is picnics taken under their shade, moonlit walks beneath their branches, and our grateful benedictions. Negligent as this might seem to the apple authorities, the trees thrive. Translated to our hillside, that means that some years a third of the apples are shot with signs of invasion, while other years, almost each apple is a hale prize. If we were marketing apples, this, of course, wouldn't do, but apples are a drug on the market in these environs, where every homestead reliquary sports as slighted and venerable an orchard as ours. Such prodigality does make one wonder about man's driven refinements.

I like to think the deer put in a good word for our apple

harvest. For the last rite we perform, as winter draws near, is to shake each branch of its remnants until the earth beneath is oozily pomaced. It doesn't take long for the deer families to stake out their claims and hold nightly banquets under their ancestral trees. Though not invited, we are well repaid.

A few years ago, we planted five dwarf fruit trees within the fenced vegetable garden, a cherry, peach, plum, pear and newfangled apple. While the others now bear beautifully, the little apple hasn't yet set a single fruit. Mike frets over it, fusses with it, glares at its barren branches. I know what's wrong. It senses somewhere in its green being that it's not really needed, knows it can't hold a candle to the grey eminences whose roots bind our earth's flesh.

A young wiseacre once told me, after a hasty tour of the place, that our trees were dying. Aren't we all, I replied, thinking of the old dreamers who plant trees they won't live to see bear. Given time's hungers, I'm grateful ours waited for me.

APOSTROPHE XII

Autumn's Prizes

Sunlight gold through golden leaves, leaf coins on the meadow. Midas strides over the hills. The pear grove path is blinding bright, paved with gold pieces and leaf lick of flame. Indian Summer.

You should *see* our foliage, say the New England kin each autumn. We have our own, I tell them, a more modest version, the colors scattered across grassy clearings and amid pines' green. Just the right amount to absorb and treasure; more would be ostentation, redundancy.

I do chores slowly, distracted by the display. On the way to the coop, the goat barn, I have to stop and pick among leaf prizes. There, that one, crimson with flecks of yellow, and this one, soft rose with green. I come back to the cabin with my buckets overflowing, and distribute my leaf harvest in every container I can find. Bowls, jars, pots and pans, in chairs even, that have sitting hollows. Way back in our early years here, when such wealth was brand new to my eyes, I spilled mounds of leaves all over the cabin floor, made where there were rugs and boards a crisp, brilliant sea. The dogs and cats thought it fine, and scampered through the woodsy carpets with high glee. Mike took a more practical view, said it was messy. A few days later, when the leaves dried and fragmented, I had to agree. I've contented myself since with the containers, with glass jarsful of gold and scarlet to set about in windows for sunlight to glance through and be multiplied.

It strikes me as a pity that the "lower" creatures (a term I dispute, but that's another subject) don't seem to take much pleasure in their homeland's panoply. The goats chew their cuds blandly season on season, impressed only by drops of rain. The dogs romp and run through the meadow whether it's snowbound or furnished by spring, its grasses somber or tawny. Fowl families—with the exception of turkeys who, I understand, gather to watch an impressive sunrise—chatter so incessantly about God knows what that they never take a minute to look around. All the cats care about is wet or dry, with never an eye to a flower or a splendid sky.

"Look, here, Sable, just look at this leaf." I shove my favorite under her Nubian face. "Notice the fine tracery, the flecks of red. . . ." Her bulging eyes stare, uncomprehending. Later, one of the dogs goes on a woods walk with me, sniffing at deer meanders, nosing out squirrel sanctuaries. From a spread of brush, he startles a family of quail. They wheel through the boughs, their wings catching glints of sunlight. I catch my breath at the sight. "Growf," the dog comments, which sounds little like, "What a lovely vision." A shame.

It's a strange thing, beauty. The eye of the beholder to the contrary, there are few who fail to be moved by a spectacular sunset, a voluptuous moonrise; few even who aren't transported by the delicacy of a flower, or etched frost on a pane. Though we might battle peevishly over this or that hand-made example, our agreement on nature's craft seems common coin.

Many feel a pensiveness about the autumn season . . . "the melancholy days," Bryant called them, "the saddest of the year." I am not one of them. I simply disbelieve winter will follow. Never mind that trees lose their bright dress day upon day, that darkness invades early evening and chill crisps the air, tomorrow will be as luminous as today, and the days after, an accumulation of the radiance which went before. Surely nature is as reluctant to give up her glory as we, surely she won't, this time, leave every tree stripped bare.

A leaf lazes by the window, looking for all the world like a ruddy snowflake of another season, a season I refuse to contemplate. It wouldn't dare.

> *The saddest of the year,*
> *Of wailing winds, and naked woods,*
> *and meadows brown and sear.*

Sunlight pale through falling leaves. Nothing stays then. Maybe the lower creatures have the right idea.

Keeping the Garden Get

Ah, the salad days of my citified youth, when I could simply rattle my cart down a grocery aisle and pick from among a vast array of vegetables, fruit, jocund juices. Never mind that they cost like sin or had dubious former lives, or even that they tasted like, well, what I thought things were supposed to taste like: sweet mush and flavored fiber.

Luckily for me, I was never one of those grown-ups whose tongue harkened back to how things used to be. My mother was an atrocious cook, and the series of family maids clove to their New England habit of overboiling and burying every victual under a glutinous sauce. I also got born just in time for the advent of boxed breakfast cereals. For years, a morning without Post Toasties was a morning misspent.

Yet, compared to my later boarding school cuisine, such bland family fare was pure haute. To this day, I can't look a cooked prune in the eye, and a basin of mashed potatoes gives my stomach the whammies. The best part about growing up and beyond all that was that I was at last in command of my own diet, freed to sup at the supermarket trough.

As it does to all mortals, such profusion eventually lost its charm. For one thing, there were our stomachs, Mike's and mine, which began misbehaving long before we aimed for a nourishing life style. For another, the quick peaks of energy gained from coffee and sweets, the relaxation from alcohol, began to sap the pool of our natural vitality and thinking matter. How hale we'd be, I began to dream, if we could grow our own veggies, eat the stuff produced by the sweat of our brow and the strain of our atrophied sinew. What *fun* it would be to preserve our own pickings, to stand over a country stove and bless with my own hand the yield; to sit down to winter meals that my own summer efforts supplied.

The nearest thing to a supermarket from our farm lies eighy-five miles and some mountain ranges away. Even if we cared to partake, for a change, of its fancies, say for old times' sake or to supplement a puny harvest, our subsistence budget forbids such extravagance. If drought or unseasonal frosts discourage our crops, it's brown rice and beans for the duration, supplemented by an occasional lettuce bought dearly (and sternly probed and weighed) in town.

The greenhouse is a lovely little place, its interior glass-bright and earth-smelling. Its six by eight A-frame accommodates an amazing amount. But it has suffered misfortune. When we first built it, we double-walled it with polyvinyl. Before summer was out, the goats had it in shreds, thinking it great sport to sneak up and nibble a hole through, then, with a purchase, tear whole sheets to tatters. The following year, Mike rebuilt the north wall with plywood, covered inside with reflective fiberglass batting. The south wall we rebuilt with old windows. A lining of plastic sheeting, stapled to the inside frame, provided three inches of dead air space. Having goat-proofed it, we then hung two heat lamps from the peak for the coldest of weathers. If Nod hadn't needed it for a sick room this last late summer, and if the November temperatures hadn't plunged to zero for a series of days when we were away, leaving the farm-sitter so busy with frozen pipes he clean forgot the heat lamps, our winter days might have been rounded by greens and tomatoes and peppers. A farm's best laid plans need faithful and minute attention. Tomorrow and tomorrow. . . .

In the meantime, the kitchen and loft windowsills groan under potted herbs; a few tiny peppers bloom on the two-year-old plant I've been loathe to waste. Beside perking up winter meals, they help keep our faith in green, and create a heartening frame to the bleak, blowsy world of midwinter.

That first garden summer without electricity was partly what determined us, by hook or crook, to get power to the premises. We'd not yet found The Great Majestic, and the toy-size cabin sink with its single spigot could scarcely accommodate one stew pot at a time, let alone a conglomerate of canning utensils and kettles. So when the harvest begged attention, the outdoor summer kitchen Mike and friends had put up came into its own. Besides a splintered picnic table, the setup held an old enamel sink whose water drained into the herb plot, and a stilt-legged, two-plate wood cookstove. That stove, I'd long ago discovered, had one cooking temperature: searing. Many a bread loaf had met incineration within its narrow confine. Still, with the only other cooking implement handy our butane campstove, the little hot box became that summer's salvation.

Because we had a scant supply of jars, I settled on the notion of freezing our vegetables, and canning only fruits, tomatoes and pickles. The first ripelings ready were the peas, delectable little morsels that burgeoned daily through July and August. Once we'd eaten our fill of them fresh, I blanched the remainder, dunked them in cool water (there was no such thing as cold, once it left the spring), and delivered them into freezer packets. Mike, standing by, would then fill a bucket with the bagfuls and dash them off to our nearest neighbor's freezer, a mile and a half down the mountain.

By the time the later vegetables ripened, we had the procedure down pat . . . as long as the weather held and the road stayed passably dry. Canning was a bit harder, involving a great shifting of bubbling pots to keep the contents and jars and juices at proper temperature all at the same time, the while stoking the hungry stove's belly to full steam ahead. Once this was done, sometimes successfully, there arose the problem of where to stash the containers in a cabin already beyond bursting its seams. Necessity, the good mother she is, forced hasty invention. Onto the cool cabin floor, beneath tables, chairs, shelves, went quart jars of the goods. They

actually looked rather pretty, the multicolored containers gleaming from the room's shadows. All one had to remember was to navigate most carefully. People who live in glass-jarred houses walk softly and leave their sticks at the door.

Despite our applied ingenuity, that was a pretty lean winter. For once autumn rains and then winter snows made their mark on the mountain, we found ourselves locked into its confines, with no earthly way to reach the contents of the freezer. Worse still, when we did manage to slip and slither down the sloppy route to retrieve a precious packet, its cargo tasted nothing like what we remembered of summer. The peas, beans and corn, prepared so carefully according to books' law, were mushy, the greens and root vegetables limp and bland. Though the long trips to and from the freezer could have done them no good, it was also an indication that I might bypass the freezing instructions and do some experimenting.

By the following harvest, we had the magic of electricity, and our freezer stood ready for its christening load. Over that past year, I had kept my ears sharp and picked up a few pointers from fellow farm women. One good cook, for example, didn't blanch corn on the cob, just shucked, bagged and froze it immediately upon picking. Another snapped her fresh-picked green beans, put them in a container of water, and froze the whole. Peas, it was said, were best shelled onto cookie sheets, quickly frozen, then bagged. If that worked, I reckoned, why not try the same method with sliced zucchini, tomatoes, carrots even? Nothing ventured, and all that. The freezer filled rapidly while I sliced and cookie-sheeted with nary a qualm.

"What if it doesn't work?" Mike asked, watching our winter cache submit to my busy knife.

"Did Ms. Einstein bug Albert?"

Well, even Einstein had a few failures. Yet most of the un-blanched, quick-frozen vegetables passed the test with flying colors. The peas and corn, even months later, were sweet and crisp, the green beans, when frozen *immediately*, were as good as new. (Those I'd let sit around for a bit picked up a grassy flavor and lost their snap.) While the zucchini and tomatoes fared equally well, the root vegetables, by and large, flunked; carrots, parsnips, beets and the like turned into a cross between mush and leather. But since they keep well for week after week in the cool darkness of the root cellar, freezing them proved superfluous anyhow.

Because the boredom of routine is my bane, I play, each year, with new ways of keeping the harvest. Last year, Mike built a five-tray food dryer, which worked such marvels with sliced apples, peaches and pears that I'm pining to try it on carrots and greens. This year, when I wearied of slicing a tub of tomatoes one frantic day, I wrapped a few whole in plastic and plunked them into the freezer. Voila! Later, after an hour's thaw, they were in perfect shape for slicing and saucing.

Since onions are usually one of our prize crops, it hurts me to lose a single bulb to rot. I seldom do any more, not since I found to my sorrow that their pretty plaits hung from kit-chen rafters were, though visually charming, ruinous to too many. The best method I've found is to hang them by their stalks in the sun—I clothespin mine to the line—until their necks are dry, then cut them from their stems and stash them in string bags nailed to root cellar beams, where they remain solid and sweet until late spring.

If there is one wisdom I've gained through my farm days, it's that while books and pamphlets, with their detailed in-structions, can encourage and guide the neophyte, they are not the final authority that experience, with a good dose of what-the-hell, can be. An example: Our second year, I pulled up the plants with still-green tomatoes by their roots, when frost threatened, and hung them, head down, plant and all, in the root cellar, where they ripened nicely clear through to December. The next year, following yet other instructions, I picked each tomato and wrapped it in tissue paper. So dressed, they ripened in the root cellar clear through to December. Following that, in my constant search for simplicity, I picked the green tomatoes from their stems and laid them loosely in root cellar boxes, where they reddened clear through to December. Who is it, I can't help but wonder, who wants to complicate things so? It's certainly not the cooperative vegetable-kind.

"Don't store potatoes and apples in the same place!" is a stricture that shouts from many a garden book page. Well, I don't know how many cellars *those* writers possess, but we're very pleased with our one, and within its bowels, apples, potatoes, onions, carrots, curing cheeses and breathing wines get along quite famously. Furthermore, my carrots are no longer stuck in damp sand, as instructions counsel, where they tended to rot, which the instructions omitted to say, but in empty buckets, which keep them far better. And our dried fruit isn't sulphured either, so there.

In confidence, I think these modifications have something to do with faith and some subtle complicity. I trust my garden's gifts to do their best by me, and they seldom fail. Though I haven't yet gotten the hang of mollifying the weather, I've an inkling that improvement lies in my own homegrown flexibility. I'm working on it. If Findhorn's gardens can break botanic strictures and defy their unfriendly clime, there but for an ear better tuned to protean nature go mine.

"Simplify, simplify!" Thoreau exhorted. It was one of his better says.

"What Did You
Put in My Cookies Now?"

Hate is too strong a word. I simply *dislike* to cook. As happy with a peanut butter sandwich as with, say, a quiche lorraine, I've never figured out what all the culinary fuss was about. It's also my contention that if the hours devoted to pre- and post-digestion were applied to more lasting pursuits, we might double the world's art and invention. On the other hand, maybe the madhouses would merely increase their folds.

If genes have anything to do with kitchen artistry, my Grandmother's must have pooled in me. She was a lovely lady, serenely in command of every activity, with never a hair out of place . . . until she entered a kitchen, a practice she avoided at almost any cost. Five feet within a cookstove's vicinity, she became a distaff Dorian Gray, her coiffure streaming, her mien in disarray. The simplest dish turned to putty in her otherwise artful hands. She was my living idol.

Be that as it may, I have learned to accept reality when it smacks its lips in my face, and the fact is, most people . . . kith and kin to the man . . . like to eat. Not just any old food, either, and not the same food day after day; not even food au naturelle, as the earth offers it, but the sorts of dishes whose fixing I consider a misuse of precious time. My own ingrate children fall into gales of laughter remembering such mementoes as Mom's apple pie, and my friends long ago learned that if they cared to ward off starvation, they had better bring their own provisions with them when they come to call, since I will be too busy talking to give eating a thought. One of the smartest ways I got around this gap in my acculturation was to marry a man who was a master of gourmandaise. One of the dumbest things I did was to vow to take on most of the cooking myself once we got into farming. That was part of the fantasy too, the rosy wife at the kitchen door, watching her mate trudge wearily back from the fields, the setting sun at his back, to a redolent and reviving farm meal. The fact of it is, Mike usually pops in from his labors mid-afternoon with, "You want me to fix dinner?"

"Oh, no," airily, "I've got it all planned."

"Really?" A note of skepticism.

"How does—um—soup and a toasted cheese sandwich sound?"

"Like lunch. I'll fix dinner."

"No, I really want to. How about, let's see, spaghetti?"

"Again? Hey, it's okay. I'll be glad to fix dinner."

"I know, a meatloaf!"

He shrugs. My meatloaves are passable, and it's been four days since the last. It's the least I can do after all his years of bending over a hot stove to whet my careless palate.

To understate, Julia Child I am not. My farm fare is unadornedly wholesome. Baked potatoes, lightly steamed vegetables, simple salads, that sort of thing. I figure if one must, ho-hum, eat, the food may as well be nutritious and as close to its original state as spoiled taste buds allow. Except for pancakes, which I do with great flourish and style. Every morning.

"Could we have boiled eggs and toast just this once?"
Mike begs from his coffee cup rim.

"My pancakes are better for you. They've got all this good
stuff in them, wheat germ, bran flakes, brewer's yeast—"

"Okay, okay, I'd rather not know."

I ask you, did Adelle Davis have to put up with this sort
of resistance? Did Irma Rombauer cook for a churl?

The first woodstove I ever encountered, I wondered aloud
where the knobs were, how one turned the curious thing on.
It didn't bode well for my lessons from our Great Majestic.
Though I loved that grand, polished nickel and proudly let-
tered behemoth the minute I saw it, it refused to return my
affection for a painfully tedious time. Measuring a vast 44"
by 30" by 56", it turned out to take ages to heat, and then
when it did, made up for its loitering ways with a fiery
fervor.

At just about the time I decided to admit defeat, plant it
with geraniums, and dig out the butane camp stove, it showed
me the hang of its secrets. Crack the stove pipe vent just so,
start food on back left plate, then shift to front middle, shift
bread around, front to back after ten minutes, then in fifteen,
cover loaves with foil, and *quick*, move that pot to left rear
plate! Cooking was no longer a bore, it was pure calisthenics
. . . to say nothing of downright calamitous to a person still
finding her way around the simplest of kitchen accoutrements. Before the G.M. and I came to an understanding, I
was beginning to resemble a posthumous Joan of Arc.

Masterful cook that he is, I must give Mike his due:
through all my trials and singed tribulations, he remained
the soul of sanguinity. Or maybe he just, long ago, resigned
himself to the scourge of my country cuisine. The only
thing that raised his patient spirit's dander . . . and does to
this day . . . was my tampering with his favorite cookies. But

I'm not a quick study. A smidgen of bone meal won't matter, and I'll put in some molasses for iron, and maybe a handful of these lecithin granules to balance those eggs. . . . I fill the cookie jar at his bedside and settle into a book and a chair, full of gladness for the nutriment I've, oh subtly, assured. Until a howl rises and spills from the loft, the sound of a creature betrayed. "What did you put in my cookies *now*???" I've no recourse. I can't blame *them* on the oven.

The Great Majestic now crowns our harvest kitchen like an ebony shrine. Though neglected in favor of the electric, sometimes for months at a time, it does not lack endearment or gratitude. More than insurance for those seasons of power failure, it is my winter comfort, my warm-hearted, trusty provider. Let the masterful cooks make their stoves a stage for their talents. Mine is a token of greener days, and a permanent sanctuary.

Nature's Thrift Store

If civilization were to crumble tomorrow, we in our hermi-
tage would somehow make do. I reflect on this sometimes,
in macabre fantasy, thinking how I'd wait for the volunteers
of last year's garden to ressurect among the weeds, how I'd
harvest their seeds ever so carefully, knowing they held the
support of all our tomorrows. But even without their provision, we'd not likely starve. There would be, barring cosmic
catacylsm, the woods' fauna and fungi and proliferous
weeds.

Our own cultivated plots support enough lamb's-quarters,
burdock and dandelion each summer to furnish the stomachs
of armies. Purslane snakes through my herbs, cous dots the
meadow's rise. In June, there are the tiny wild onions to dig
from the rocky slopes of the northern hillside, and in August,
along our creek's rise, airy pink heads of wild garlic nod. And
then there's the pond some two miles up-mountain where
redwings and cattails multiply spring after spring.

Let me tell you a common tale. Some years back, a couple
visited the farm with dog-eared copies of Euell Gibbons
tucked into their knapsacks. Which of these edibles did our
environs boast, they wanted to know, and could we help find
them, and hold a wild foods feast? The garden seeming too
mundane a start, we took them up to our secret woods places,

where we urged them to fill their buckets with wild miner's lettuce, watercress from the seeps, vetch pods and solomon's seal, wild currants for sweets, and mint from the streamsides for tea. Because it was between mushroom seasons, we ended the grocery spree at the cattail pond, mucking about amid the objections of redwings, pulling up stalks by the armsful. That evening, we four sat down to the banquet. The miner's lettuce salad, tossed with a touch of wild onion bits and lamb's quarter, was a mild success, and Mike's watercress soup got a bit of a rave. The tiny vetch peas didn't go very far though, and when we got to the cattail stalks, steamed and buttered to delectation, the woman's face fell.

"What's *this*?"

Mike explained, adding, as a selling point, that it was also called Russian asparagus.

"Then what is *that*?" her companion asked, pointing to a platter of mixed greens.

"Pigweed and nettles with a garnish of wild parsley seeds," I told him. He took a tentative nibble and smothered a shudder.

"My teeth feel funny," he said.

"It's the greens, and what your teeth feel is clean."

In a show of country bravado, Mike and I polished off the rest of the fare while our guests busied themselves with elaborate silverware play. Surely things would improve, I thought, when I served my cattail flour biscuits with wild currant jelly. They didn't, much, though polite remarks reigned.

Much later, halfway into dreams, we heard a commotion, doors slamming, a tiptoed board's creak. I got out of bed to investigate. There were the two of them, their heads buried in the refrigerator. My stifled giggle announced my intrusion. Caught red-handed, they blushed and stared.

"Oh, I hope you don't mind," the woman stammered.

"We were just, uh, trying to find a bite of bread, and maybe some cheese."

"Darn, we're fresh out. But I do have a few cattail biscuits left, and a bowl of fresh greens." Oh, I can be mean.

Yet we ourselves aren't wild food aficionados, having found that for us, there's a time and a place for their reaping. Like spring, when the very tongue hungers for green, or during gardening, when lamb's-quarters picked and nibbled on the spot is a delicacy. If our lives depended on foraging, we'd doubtless survive. I'd probably grumble a lot, ingrate that I'd be, because the deer beat me to the wild berries and the birds plucked the currants and just-ripe chokecherries clean. Most of all for the fact that roasted dandelion root, no matter how you cut it, does *not* taste any closer to coffee than pine-sap to Wrigley's finest.

But in case crusty Euell is listening from his lush Elysium, I do want to speak up for the *pièce de résistance* of earth's bounty, the mushroom. Understand, I'm no expert. I leave that up to Mike, with his tomes and his careful spore studies, possessions to which I might very well owe my life. We have, both in our woods and a stone's throw from urban blight, found a mind-boggling variety, a fraction of which he has identified as safely edible. He is no fun at all. Stumbling through fir shadows and decayed tree mold, we have come across a few specimens no guide book deigns to cover.

"Mike, look what I found, it's a giant! By itself it would make a whole feast."

Squint-eyed, he turns it over, examines its gills and volva, breaks a piece to see how it colors. "Umm, I dunno. We'll take it home and see what the spore pattern indicates."

"Aw, come on, just *smell* it, it smells delicious!"

"That's got nothing to do with it. Now put it carefully into a separate bag."

"Tell you what, why don't I just take the tiniest nibble, just a thumbnail's worth couldn't hurt. . . ."

"Joanie!" He blanches and takes my treasure. Oh, enterprise, where is thy spirit?

There are, bless our earth mother, a few sure-fire, no-fail sorts of fungi which the pickiest, Mike among them, can gather and feast on without first crossing themselves with a prayer. Of these, morels are the pinnacle. Once you've seen one, they're unmistakable; once you've tasted one, sautéed or stuffed, you are happy to die. (Of natural causes, morels being indisputably benign.) Then after the morels have fruited and perished in their dappled fir groves, if the summer is neither too dry nor soggy, the boleti burst forth. One

year, the season was so perfectly nourishing for their needs, we stumbled over them in every woods' shade, their pancake-like crowns pushing up through the duff, their spongy undersides velvet to our touch.

"Oh, Lord," Mike would groan at the next pine-trunk turn, "there are more of them."

"Well, we can't let them waste. You'll be glad for them come winter." So we filled yet another bag to overflowing and hiked back with our packs and canvas totes looking like Santa's stores. Luckily, genus Boletus dries to perfection. Once we've eaten them beyond our fill, minced fresh and sautéed, we pop them, sliced, into the dehydrator and go about our farm business. No winter soup, stew or omelet would be complete without a garnish of their crisp remains.

Early summer's clavaria dry equally well, though we seldom give them much chance to. Coming across their undersea shapes in the woods' recesses is like striking gold. One doesn't want to hang onto the wealth, but spend and enjoy. Oyster mushrooms, on the other hand, are a fungal happy medium. So many of them palm out from the cottonwoods along the creek banks that we can both gorge them at meals and pack the drying screens with their surplus. An old tree stump in a town flower garden is our favorite source; they spread across and down its trunk in enormous dimension, pearl-colored, silken, succulent. On the drive home, I hold a choice piece to my nose, savoring the damp, slightly salt-sea smell, wondering about the simple and complex invention that urged them out of the ghost of that tree.

Come September, we begin hoping for early fall rains, that puddles might wet the woods' earthen roadsides where shaggy mane spores lie in wait. More often than not, the jet stream obliges, and winter preparations must be put aside for the harvest. Where one pale, priapic shape thrusts up one day, whole legions emerge by the next. They cannot be ignored. If the picker isn't hasty on the spot, their solid bodies turn gelatinous and black, taking the shape and look of a beggarman's tattered umbrella. It doesn't do to be greedy, either, for the lot has to be gotten home to wash and slice and sautée (with a dash of sherry and marjoram) and put in the freezer before auto-digestion moves upon them. I solve this hazard in a minor way by eating much of my pick right from the roadside, dirt-crust and all. That they're not, raw and pungent, to everyone's taste is beyond my understanding. So is the overdosed stomachache I nurse into the night.

Other sorts of mushrooms make their homes nearby; great fist-size puffballs, their tops faceted like diamonds, and tiny, cone-hatted *panaeolus,* and the upside-down crown-shaped *peziza.* One year we found a circle of deep purple *lepista nuda* in an abandoned corral, and I ate so many and got so sick I was sure they'd comprised my last meal. Another season, a friend went woods tramping and came back with her billowed skirt full of deadly amanita. When Mike buried them and suggested she scrub her hands, she was somewhat put out. So was I. I had wanted to dry a few and keep them as reserve weapons for emergencies like visitors overstaying their welcomes or hunters who savage our wildlings. Mike says there are laws. He is no fun at all.

It was bandied about for ages that edible mushrooms had no nutritive value. I didn't mind; neither does candy, and I frequently fall prey to its charms. Recently, though, there is news that the delectable fungi do, after all, nourish. I'm not surprised. The deer eat them, the goats find them tasty, and their palates are wiser than mine. It's good to know, too, that should we ever be driven to forage for our survival, the mushroom would help sustain us. Given an occasional dish of my favorites, I could face Armageddon with a dash of sherry, marjoram and savoir faire.

Meditation

on a Mushroom

It isn't just the season or even the confines of weather that signal the time. It's more the look of the sky on a day not much different than others, a drift of warm, piney air from across the green curve of meadow. One of us will look up from a chore, sniff, notice maybe that the blue field iris are fading, and shout as though blessed by a vision, "Let's go moreling!"

I'm not sure there is such a word, "moreling." There should be, a term kin to "berrying," "fishing," calling up as they do a scent of endeared, hidden places, the slant of the sun there, the drift of the shadows, the earth shape. It might be because of its tenuous nature that the hunt for morels is the most cherished rite of all, and one charged with the highest anticipation. Fish dart, barring man's meddling, in the same streams year upon year, and the hardy wild berries burst forth from the same bushes on annual schedule. But there's a rub to a good morel harvest. The succulent, secretive sprouts demand a delicate balance of warmth and moisture to push through the dappled woods' floor and to flourish there in their short shrift of given days.

Up here in our Oregon Blues, morel season can fall any

time from early May til mid-June. If spring has been dour and the earth too long in warming, nary a sign of the fluted cones will emerge. If the weather heats up too quickly and the forest floor withers dry, the recalcitrants will consider it the better part of valor to refuse issue at all. Such fussy habits make this crown of mycophagy the more precious, their discovery the more beatific. If old Martial was right in pronouncing the early fruits as most esteemed, then those that bloom but now and then, and if and only, harbor secrets begetting of miracles. So even when the weathers flounder and the seasonal signs appear gloomy and foreboding, we are driven one late spring day to the high woods where the firs thrive, just to see, just in case, just for old times' sake, and to work up, if we skunk, a halfheartedly blasphemous mourning. "Not one," we sigh to each other, after hours of tramping and zealous scrutiny. "Not even one, damn this devious weather!"

But nature compensates her faithful. There are the good years, those with a spring measured by a span of warm days and a scatter of showers, years when each May and June freshet-to-torrent is counted and blessed, and each day the wood stove is let rest from after breakfast until dark increases the promise. Never mind that the paths goo and gumbo and it's too wet to plant; the mycelium, veining out under the duff, needs the moisture. And just feel the sunshine this morning; surely the timid morels will take courage beneath its grace.

So the proper day comes, untallied but felt, and one of us bells out the message. The hoe is left standing mid-garden, the fence wire where the stray cows breached is let dangle mid-air. Old buckets and worn knives are gathered, and we head, trying to look nonchalant, like kids playing hooky, for the deep wood above the slant of our mountain.

Each fir grove has its name now, private names given them last year and the year before and the one before that. There is Happy Birthday, where we found our first feast on Mike's fifty-fourth, and Bellwether, where the first small nubs often indicate the extent of the harvest to come. Little Punkin is named for our female hound, after the time she accompanied us there as a pup and promptly got lost stalking a butterfly. Joanie's Hot Spot needs no explication, nor does Elk Hollow or Porcupine Ridge. But Lookout Meadow, Flat Tire Bend and Ent Hill are no more, lost now to the woodcutters' hungers. We try not to dwell on the plunder, a minor sin in the lumbermen's mania. Instead, each year we extend our hunting grounds, and pray for a safer woods keeping.

Friends invited up for a morel feast often beg to share our quests. We let them, sometimes, reluctantly, but it's never the same. People talk in the woods, shout things to each other.

They don't seem to know that the deep, holy silence is part of the pleasure, seem unaware they can't hear bird call or bough whisper above their compulsive commotion. They trample, unseeing, on clumps of violet and wood sorrel, and sometimes, despite our warnings, pick a rare venus slipper or pine drop, unable to let beauty just be.

No, it is better alone. We have learned to soften our footfall, to stop still and watch the eagle soar from her tallest pine, where she circles over until she's assured we are as clumsily grounded as we seemed to be. We've learned, above all, that it's not just morels we're in search of, but that they are a bonus, and the excuse we need to drop our spring chores and leave garden rows, to find a more nourishing sustenance than any harvest could offer.

The woods are always there, and within blessed reach. If it weren't for the promise of their springtime bounty, we might put off reacquaintance with their deeper places too long, might let the blurred detail of renewal pass at our chore-rapt backs. We never come home empty-handed. Buckets morel-laden or light, what we return with is the senses' and spirits' provision, fresh and fortified.

IV

BEYOND SUBSISTENCE

Not by Bread Alone

Money. Such a foolish thing. Pieces of paper and metal that can make or break lives, whole families' well-being. Yet there is no escaping its bonds, even in the simplicity of an abundant mountain habitation.

We hadn't intended to be as churchmouse poor as we've, countrified, been, hadn't meant to take the sub of subsistence so literally. When we settled in here, though we had a small cache set aside for emergencies and major supplies, our main source of income was to be the home we had sold, whose payments would trickle in regularly through the following decade. If we could market our crafts now and then, we considered, we'd have mad money to spend.

But fate's capricious urn had other things in store, for what purpose other than to test our resolution and ingenuity, I can't imagine. Tempted to beat our brows and beg the skies, "Why us?," we have forced ourselves instead beyond the churlish circumstances of our undoing. We got, in total, three payments before the deal fell to a tide of bankruptcy amidst a web of real estate complexities which caused legal wizards to pull at their beards and fall victim to tics. Worse, our property, our once beloved home, was lost.

So the mad money to be made by our wits became our sole source of subsistence, inflation having supped at the dregs of

the cache. Living on the brink of poverty, weighing each
grain of feed and wisp of hay, avoiding doctors and dentists
at any cost short of terminal pain is neither easy nor insur-
mountable. One adjusts. One pretends he or she is a true pioneer, unaware of the outer world's markets and access to ease.
One pulls the shawl of her mountain about her, trusts to
nature, plumbs the reaches of her capabilities. One beats her
brow sometimes, and implores the skies, "Why *me*?"

Letters reach us seasonally from unknowns, friends of
friends, or people who have read one or a few of our essays.
"Is homesteading still possible?" they ask. "We've been
stashing country money from city jobs," they say. "Do you
think we're ready to try?" They're not easy to answer from
our personal blind. I'd hate to lead country dreamers astray
with a rose-colored view, or frighten them off with the skele-
ton of reality. And down at the very base, I know environment is shaped in one's head, and that farm success feeds
on one's strength and resiliancy, qualities hard to measure
until they are sorely tested.

It is alarming to see that the local farmers who hold less
than, say, 600 fertile acres, can no longer survive, how they
dream of selling parcels to weekenders and moving to town,
or, if they're still full of years, to the job-lean metropolis. It
used to be that a son would be happy to inherit his father's
160, that all he required were a family shelter and a plot of
viable land. But that was before the advent of the R.V., the
air-conditioned tractor cum tape deck, the chore-free dish-
washer and dryer and microwave oven; before even insurance became mandatory, and taxes soared exponentially
each time an urbanite bought a few acres for his sometime
playground.

A young forest worker we know looks at his elderly parents' 160 and scratches his head. "I dunno what to do with

it when they're gone," he says. "I can't support my family on 160 acres, probably not even on 1000, these days."

He's right, of course. His daughter has her own car, his son a motorcycle. His house in town boasts two color TV's, and outside in the driveway, there's a cabover camper with four bikes and a boat for its cargo. I'm sure it strikes him and his neighbors as weird that someone like us would give up such rewards to adopt the life-style they themselves have struggled beyond. If they could see our bank balance, they'd *know* we were plumb crazy. As we are. Sane, stable people don't take vows of poverty to hard-scrabble on an isolated, tumble-down farm. Yet the number of the loony and city-liberated is swelling; small, marginal farms are finding new life under soft, eager hands, and the old-time cabin crafts flourish. The gift of life, some are finding, is not just a flourish of ribbons tying a fancy box.

I wish mightily that someone would survey the number of us first-time farmers, tabulate the successes and failures among us and study their causes. Most of those Noble Experiments we've observed have ended as tales of woe. Like the fellow who took a job teaching at a country school, but was fired in short order when he let his beard and tresses grow. (Principle counted heavily with him, and he found it hard to accept a culture of such narrow judgment.) Another got a job at the mill, while his wife and son carried the husbandry burden. They managed well until the mill closed and he became just one of many seeking re-employment. And there was the couple who thought they could support their new farm by driving the school bus, unaware that in a rural community where jobs are like hen's teeth, newcomers are the last to be hired . . . and then, only peevishly; and the

young nursing mother, who toiled so endlessly she con-
tracted mono, and the baby got sick, and the medical bills
ate up all her farm savings.

Seen at a distance, it isn't so much *events* that make the
difference between surmounting and going under, and sheer
luck is too rare to consider. At the bottom, it's attitude. One
new farm family we know has suffered a series of calamities
that would drive a saint from his shrine. The deer ate their
first garden to the ground, then destroyed their dwarf fruit
tree grove; the cow died in labor, the calf was stillborn; the
second cow strayed off for days, and in looking for her, they
crashed their truck in a hidden ravine; the replacement calf
broke her leg the same week coyotes ate half of their chickens. Their daughter can't get to school in bad weather because
the road is in such poor condition, and because of that abo-
mination, their Jeep frequently gives up the ghost.

Without electricity or a phone, often stranded by vehicle
trouble, the five of them crowded into a nutshell of a shelter,
they love every minute of their new country life, and shrug
off each misfortune as easily as one scratches an itch. When
their money runs low, he gets a job plumbing for someone, or
doing repairs. When one rig suffers calamity, they borrow
a part from another and patch it together. Only two years out
of the city, they give the lie to the legends of greenhorns,
and put *us* to shame. Yet these are no idealogues intellectual-
izing the return to nature, the forfeiture of the marketplace;
they are indominable, pliant, determined, and perhaps most
important of all, they have deep wells of humor. Laughter,
then, might be an essential, the great leveler of farm tribula-
tion, the renewer of energies endlessly spent. If we couldn't
find a core of drollery in our fumbling attempts, or jest
back at the japes of nature, all the king's treasure would avail
us an empty prosperity.

So here we dig in on our mountain, wondering if the post-

An awareness of kismet is handy when you fall head over heels for a place.

Love is famously myopic. An endeared, be it person or parcel, can seem on the surface to be capable of filling all one's physical and psychic needs, only to turn out to be a recluse and miser. "It's as easy," my Grandmother was fond of saying, "to love a banker as a ne'er-do-well gypsy." I listened, but I knew all along where my gypsy heart lay.

It would be just as easy, no doubt, to love a more provident place than our wilderness aerie, a place with access to markets where we might barter our wares and farm surplus. It wouldn't be easy to pull up roots bedded in joy and pain. A farm grows on you the way favorite old clothes take your measure and shape. Someone else knew it, old John Carl, who built this place, and who, when his cupboard went bare, got deranged, a better escape, to his way of thinking, than deserting the orchard and the tall boarded cabin whose roof brushed the heavens. Lest our fortunes follow, we stop now and then and consider the options.

"The land was ours before we were the land's." Robert Frost knew, too. Hold on, John Carl, we're on our way.

APOSTROPHE XIII

Spring Do-Lists

One day with a semblance of spring, and I suddenly note out the window the mess winter has left in its wake, the jobs we didn't manage to finish before the sun turned ruthlessly southward. There is the porch with no steps to it, and the fence that's all bent out of shape, and the warped greenhouse door, and the clothesline trailing the ground where the dogs yanked drying towels for play. And the wood stove needs cleaning out and the washroom window is busted and the chicken coop roost has come loose from the wall. Better make a list before I forget, and then another, arranging priorities.

My accumulated lists, tucked into dark niches when they turn tattle-tale, could paper the walls of a good-sized abode. There are wish lists made up from the catalogues, lists of books I want to read, and in what order, friends I want to write, bills I mean some day to pay. The good thing about list-making is it makes you feel you're accomplishing something, while deferring the duties it outlines. For a while. But there comes an inevitable reckoning, when someone falls off the stepless porch, when seedlings overtake kitchen sills and the greenhouse isn't fixed, when ashes disgorge from the neglected stove, and the clothes have to be washed twice because they've trailed from the sagging line into the mud. And, oh yes, the chickens are sneaking through the gap in the garden fence, probably in retribution for the sea-sickening sway of their roost. Spring do-lists are always the longest of all.

Mike strides in from his workshop to change to a cooler shirt. "What are you doing?" he asks, with more than a touch of suspicion.

"Oh, just scribbling some stuff." But he knows. By dinner, he'll find a large piece of paper set unsubtly in front of his plate, a paper whose heading says something like "Now that April's here," or "Solstice suggestions." (I'm not good at guile.) And he'll sigh and set it aside. It's getting dark, and, well, maybe tomorrow we'll discuss it. Right now we have to compare today's counts of wild geese, and after that, fix a box for the new kittens. Yes, tomorrow, maybe.

But tomorrow arrives, and it is snowing. You can't even see the hole in the fence for the flakes, and if I avoid the root cellar I won't get dripped on where the snow melts through the gap in the door. I review my list, feeling both grateful and maddened. There's something wrong there. Too sternly compulsive, and for all its length, I've left the most important stuff out. I sit down in front of the grey-spectred window and take a new piece of paper.

> Look at crocus
> Watch robins
> Take a woods walk
> Pick bouquet of buttercups
> Read spring poem
> Sit in sun (at least one hour)
> Study seed packet pictures

it says. I consider it, then add one more item:

> Tear up first list.

Man does not live by chores alone.

A Day in the Life of....

The deer breached my herb plot last night, then topped off the garnish with a few plump dooryard tomatoes. Or was it the goats, yesterday, when I was tending the lame drake? No, the goats were downhill then, where I'd chased them after they'd nibbled the peony and beheaded the pansies. I wouldn't have been so stern if I hadn't just discovered that the porcupines had broken a branch off the plum before the she-dog discovered their felony and got six more quills in her snout defending the grove.

So I spent the morning in mourning; those tomatoes, the first to ripen, and the parsley and fennel, all ferny and lush. But there was no time for funk. We had to get busy and psych the dog so we could sneak up and pull quills before she went into a fit. I manged to grab three with the pliers before she trounced Mike's hand. Midmorning, bedecked with Band-Aids, he went off to the woods for surcease and to gather winter wood.

The cabin swept, I went outside and turned on the faucet to rinse out the chickens' feed bucket. The faucet gurgled, spat and went silent. With a plea to the heavens, I checked the hoseline for kinks. The spring couldn't have dried up that suddenly, drought or no drought. Yet the hose was smooth all the way . . . and decidedly empty. The goats trailed me uphill while I checked the half-buried conduit for leaks. They butted and pranced with not a care in the world. "Worry!" I ordered them. "You may have drunk your last drink." Their bells clamoured cheerily in a game of horn tag.

No leaks, but the pipe ran into an empty spring tank. The sun beat down hot, and I wished I had bathed that morning, before the waters vanished forever. I should try to find Mike, I thought. But, no, let him have his last peaceful hour. The woods will give him strength for this ordeal. Plunking down on the prickly weeds, I pictured the corn ripening gold in its husks, now on its way to dying, visioned my bean tendrils shriveling from green to rust, my squashes sinking into a shell of their former selves.

The Bible, that might help. Country women historically found balm in its pages. Where *was* that old family book? I ran down the hill, hoof and bell-trailed, and into the cabin to scan the bookshelves. Damn! What comfort could Steinbeck, Durrel, even Vonnegut offer me now? Back out to the workshop, to scour the unkempt tool shelves where spare books spilled among egg cartons and a clutter of implements awaiting repair. Ahh, The Holy Bible, there beside the wasp's nest. A Psalm would be nice.

> *And God made the rivers to run . . .*
> *He giveth waters to restore . . .*

Balm? Salt to the wounds! And I'm thirsty, and the chickens are scratching in the poppies again, and where is that dog, her hen-herding shirked? Under the porch, it comes to me, nursing her quill wounds and pride.

Mike returns, his face flushed and damp. I put on a brave countenance. "The spring's dried up," I announce with just a touch of drama.

"Whaaa . . ? It can't be!" He dashes off to retrace my pipe examination. The goats follow, retracing their hike. What fun, their bounding proclaims. Back down, grim-faced, Mike announces, "Tank's empty." I nod. So am I. Wordlessly, we track the downhill pipeline toward the garden. Almost to the fenceline, we muck into a mud hole, hear the sound of water trickling. The color comes back to Mike's face. He stoops to mend the detached elbow, then rises like Moses.

After we've walked the pipeline, bouncing out air bubbles, I set about watering the dooryard flowers. A yellow jacket sidles up and attacks my leg "Ow!" I yowl, clutching the bite. "Ow!" Mike joins from the porch, where the dog is defending her muzzle against his quill prying.

Mid-afternoon, I take time from weed-pulling to feed the flocks. The recuperating dog emerges from under the porch to perform her bounden duty of chasing the chickens from each peaceful corner into their yard. While I fend off the bedlam of ruffled feathers, the goats catch up and butt me playfully through the gate. No eggs today; six hens squat their sitters stubbornly over their nests, intent on brooding. The coop is a swarm of bees, and upon investigation, I find them massed gluttonously over a broken shell. Flailing at their congregation, I hurriedly fill the grain tray. The goats climb in beside me and begin to munch. The setting hens warm up a warning of imminent chaos. "Out, Sable!" I command, swatting her rump. Tylwyth joins her, and the hen commotion increases. "Tylwyth, outside!" Smack. I shove Sable's butt out the door and Tylwyth shoves me from behind. A chicken snickers.

Aha, there's an egg in the goat manger the dogs overlooked. Tomorrow's breakfast bodes cheerier. Mike runs by me, panting, "Smoke, over in the east forty!" I look up and see a grey spiral rising above the far trees. Where *is* that patrol plane? It's past due. Before I can catch up, Mike is into the truck and gone. His dust billow grits my eyes . . . or is it, Lord help us, smoke? Should I follow him, or get on the phone? I sniff the air. Acrid. My heart chokes my throat. All those ponderosas, all that dry pine duff, and the meadow nothing but tinder grass now. Before I can take a step in either direction, the truck returns. "Hager's burning slash," Mike says, slamming the door hard. "It's farther off than I thought, past our boundary. *Dumb* time to burn, we'd better keep our eye on it."

For the rest of the afternoon, my eyes remain glued to the east, until finally, before dusk falls, the smoke spiral shrinks and drifts off like an ambling ghost. The ducks nag from the pond that I have forgotten their rations.

Evening, a full moon rising. While dinner bubbles on the stove, we sit on the porch, drinking in the cool air, and red wine from jelly glasses. The goats are milked and bedded, the chickens locked for the night. The spent dog sleeps at our feet, resting up for new porcupine missions. A bell chimes in the orchard, then another. "The goats are out!" I exclaim. Mike rises, sighing, and follows me down the hill. "*Got* to fix that gate," he mutters.

By the time we're back, the goats scolded and coaxed, the dinner is scorched and bees sup our deserted wine. A bat dips across the moon's face and the crickets take up their chorus. I lean against the post, listening. "Perfect evening," I murmur.

"Mmm, nice day, too," Mike breathes, his eyes on the moon-silvered meadow.

Funny thing is, we mean it.

Hurt Not the Earth...
Nor the Trees*

There's little car traffic on the road to town, little on any road in this sparse expanse. What does ply the corrugated pavements and graveled byways is a fleet of gargantuan log rigs laden with fat lengths of fir trunks or gravity-defiant piles of cut lumber. They grind up the piney hills and down into the hairbreadth valleys as though they possessed the world, their drivers tooting, grinning, gunning like power-mad kings. Sometimes you get a whiff of woodsap when they volley past, a last breath of the plundered forest. I try to avert my eyes from their cargo, try not to picture the wrack such harvests leave where there towered green spires. It is hard. Our land lies in the middle of those woods the timbermen reap. It is hard.

My sorrows for the warred-on woods are kept secret, and must remain so if I am to live in peace with my neighbors. Lumber means jobs, means money. The villages scattered alongside the rivers, the settlements connivent with huge mills are tied umbilically to timber. It is a marginal existence, one which deems itself under constant threat from the nature

_____

* Revelation

crazies. If you want to get into trouble in a local bar, try remarking to the leather-shouldered, hard-hatted imbibers how sad it is to see a woods defiled. There are no better ways to cause a commotion. Trees? Gawdalmighty, there's a million of 'em. Besides, doesn't the company replace what's cut with tree farms? Yes, the company tries hard to. The company in these parts tries to be law-abiding, priding itself on the good woodsmanship of its ways. And the trees still fall, those ancient godheads, under a siege of greed their decades never saw.

(In my dreams, the trees plot revenge beneath co-conspiring stars, murmur of the time they'll march on their destroyers. With mighty heaves, they pull roots from the soil and advance in lumbering legions, their branches flailing toward a deadly hug. In my dreams, small men are crushed like flotsam, left splintered where they slept beside their saws.)

A trifling creek runs past the bottom of our meadow. When we first made our home above it, it was an idyll. Tall firs and pines reached above its banks, their boughs giving shade to fingerling pools. We often walked its shores, or simply found a fallen log to sit and watch from, nursing daydreams silver, green. One morning the silence of our hillside was broken by the sound of motors, and then the drone of chain saws. The racket rose to our cabin from the virgin creek's meander. It went on for days, while we stood at the top of our meadow and listened, stood bowed and still, like the bereaved at a graveside.

Weeks later, long after the din had moved on to tear the silence of more distant groves, we steeled our spirits to go view the aftermath. The streamside was a no-man's-land. Broken logs crisscrossed like tumbled matchsticks, limbs wattled the banks. The sun glared unimpeded on murky waters, the birds that once filled boughs with trilling celebrations were still; in mourning, probably, or frightened away. In our aching souls, we were glad the birds were missing. Human, we were ashamed. It was illogical, the way we felt about it . . . broken, like the limbs. There was still a wealth of untouched woods nearby, still oases of frond shade where one could make believe in Rima, Ent folk, the Findhorn sprites, where the senses could get lost in bird call, and the corner of one's eye catch darting squirrels. Still places even where elk herds gathered at meadows' edges and deer rumps flagged amid the columns' shadows. On borrowed time, though, every driven being. What good is a Venus slipper, a fawn or eaglet, weighed against man's inclinations? I'll tell you how they're measured in these parts, in the words of one of our forest experts: "Trees are there to be cut." What price dominion?

We should get blinders, I guess, to wear on our woods journeys. Just last week I noticed blue marks on the trunks of my most cherished grove, the site where we find our first spring mushrooms, and where in the deepest recesses, deer have made their pine duff nurseries. By a shady seep there you can smell such earth smells, loamy and pungent, that your very breath grows heavy, and you know how earth *feels* to the roots that feed there, to the secret creatures buried there alive. Blue marks on the trunks now. It won't be long.

(In my dreams I battle for the trees, brave for their being and careless of mine. I throw myself under invading earth movers, offer my limbs to an army of saws. "You'll touch this wood over my dead body!" I bellow. Magic incantations bless my tongue as I speak for the tongueless earth holders. The woodsmen back off in wonder, leaving their saws to rust in peace.)

Maybe I'd feel better if I knew where all that wood went, to what end the trees were commodity. I doubt it. Ticky-tack

structures in suburbia, someone's fence to wall out the neighbors, a poolroom cosmetic. What manbeast of prehistory was the first to slay a tree for his abode? Why couldn't the cretin stick to mud and stone, why didn't he lift his eyes to the uplifting branches, run his crude hand over the trunk flesh and feel fellow force flowing there? Why couldn't he foresee whole mountains denuded, the pyres of boughs proclaiming the greed of his heirs? Whoever the benighted soul might have been, may he wander in a treeless limbo, rueful for the memory of shade.

It is said more primitive people cure their ailments by hugging a tree. I believe it. There is strength there, and silent empathy; an exchange of . . . something. Even the most stunted offers solace to a spirit dinned by human nonsense, and to walk through a pine woods in summertime is to cleanse the breath of all its manmade poisons. As woods offer ample fare for their wildlings, they tender us tame folk more than we know.

"There's some good trees there you could harvest," said the realtor when we bought our acres. Someone did once, long ago. Huge stumps are scattered on our hillsides and hollows. They make good sitting places when we're hiking-weary, places to rest and look around at their heirs. I'd rather have the grand old trees though, rather look out from the hill-top and watch their sky communion. None of the remainder will reach such sublime proportion in my lifetime, and beyond that, there are no guarantees.

(In my dreams, my spirit hovers over the woods I misname mine, for an eternity. I cast a spell on the multitude, protecting them from greed's dictation. Owls home forever among the dusky branches, deer slip beneath bough-crossed moon-rise; jays flit and jaw from storied limbs, as did their skyblue parents' parents. The cabin is but a pile of boards, the garden a grassy bier. The spelled trees thrive and stand.)

If I have my way, I will be buried beneath one of their kind, the old apple, maybe, where I like to climb. It pleases me to think of my mortal clay thumped with windfalls, my bones being brushed by a homing root. I won't need a gravemarker, but someone might carve, below my initials, Hurt Not This Tree. There are lesser legacies.

Country Invention
and Storybook Farms

Why was it, I once wanted to know, that those farms beyond the junction at Kimberly were so tidy and neat? Those farmers live nearer to town, a neighbor explained, and could run into shops for fixin's whenever there rose a need. Humph, I thought, from the haunt of an urban esthetic, ours would stay trim and exemplary.

You should see it today.

Perched on a shelf of the hillside, the working area looks best under winter's habiliment, the dogs' retrieved bones roundly buried, and the trash heap the goats forage a mysterious mound. Early summer is good too, when the lush meadow and apple blossoms distract the eye from the stuff spilling out of the logshed, the lumber and steel scraps banked in the yard, the buckets and seed flats lined up like good soldiers beside the porch barrack.

"Got to get this place cleaned up," Mike declares one April day.

"Uh-*huh*, it's a shambles. If anyone came to visit I'd be mortified."

So we start with the logshed, that catch-all for busted gear and empty cartons, that graveyard of tattered feed sacks and basket case fishing gear, tossing the amalgam out into the yard for sorting, scrutinizing, and decisions to hang onto the residue for just one more year. But just when the stuff is well aired and gathered into a pile, a day dawns that is perfect for planting the greenhouse, a day when the packets of seeds seem to sit up and take note of the balmy, ripening air. And after the seeds are bedded, there's the granary to patch and the goat barn to muck out, and the spring tanks must be drained and cleaned of their winter detritus.

But even when the logshed and other embarrassments are whipped into shape, the farm is a long way from spic and span. The scrap heaps aren't just a season's accumulation or the result of a careless ordering, they are the reserves of ma-

terials no farm can function without: buckets of bolts and
screws and tool handles, scraps of aluminum flashing, sec-
tions of stove pipe and hoses, nozzles and saw blades and
inner tube pieces for patching, and old sinks and frayed nets
and frozen stiff spigots and cart wheels and wheelless wheel-
barrows. The fecund heaps multiply, season on season. Busted refrigerators and freezers whose offer we couldn't turn
down, old Singer bases, and the eviscera of motor vehicles
crowd the once virgin slopes, tucked and shoved against the
backs of outbuildings, trying to hide their ill features under
tarps or behind jerry-built boards. As much as I'd cherish a
storybook farm, I know that what a blood bank is to a bleed-
er, such accumuli are to a farm's operation. There is no hard-
ware store down the street, no repair person to run to when
equipment fails. For the want of a shoenail, a day or a week
could be squandered.

Yet I am a tidy sort, and every so often, living hard by a
junk heap rankles. "Mike, look what the goats have dragged
out. Do we *have* to keep this old thing?"

"My air filter? You're damn right we do. That's what I'm
going to make my crawdad trap out of."

"Okay, but what about these bicycle wheels I keep tripping
over?"

"Those are to go on the garden cart when I get around to
it. We could get rid of that coal hod, though. The bottom's
all rusted."

"The heck we can, I'm going to reline that someday and
make a super wastebasket."

The coal hod still sits in its rusty limbo, but Mike did indeed fashion the crawdad trap from the filter, and caught a
batch of dads and two clumsy snakes on its trial run. And one
of the cast-off fridges is now a smoker, with an antediluvian
Maytag tub for its firebox. A heavy wire spool is our tablesaw
table, and a wheelless barrow the barnyard water basin. An

old steel file drawer makes a handy cat box; a discarded fan circulates the dehydrator's air and its thermostat is an old frypan control. The barbecue spit motor rescued from the dump runs our cheese paddle, the barbecue pan is a birdbath. Grinders, buffers, sanders, themselves fabricated from discards, are powered by obsolete washing machine motors.

But these are mere nuts and bolts in contrast to the white elephants we have stashed about, hidden as best they can be in woods' shelters so as not to offend the hillside's tag-end sensibilities. We talk sometimes of selling the camper we lived in while rebuilding the cabin, until we remember the catch-all burden it holds. What an eyesore!

One year we'll build a barn, maybe, and have room for storage. I've a feeling it will fill quickly, and as soon overflow. But what a picnic the resident goats will have, picking over the booty, conquering rust mountains because they are there. Trash grows on you, in a place where it's also treasure. It can only be storybook people who keep storybook farms. I wonder what the Waltons' dog does with *his* cache of bones, and where *they* store their old mower blades?

There is, though, a breadth between practical rusticity and outright squalor. The worst urban ghetto would be hard pressed to match a handful of homesteads down yonder, places where wrecks of bygone vehicles lie askew in farmyards, and rusty tools wallow like scuttled ships. Such sites more often than not sport one or two patched-up trailers, perched like lifeboats above the sea of surrounding cadavers. We are tempted to shield our eyes when we pass the offending spreads, but we dare not. The rag-tag farmer's pigs and chickens are likely to be lying in wait around the next bend, plotting a saunter out onto the road just when we think we're home free. Yet in searching my battered esthetic, I have to admit that I'd choose such rural eyesores any day over those lifeless, citified "ranch-style" abodes, their lawns and plants manicured to perfection, their concrete driveways pristine, which dot the more prosperous reaches of our river valley. Nature herself is not always neat. She is never contrived.

There was an earlier time when we thought of lining the meadow driveway with poplars, of landscaping the cabin-side yard; of fussing, "improving." I realize now that would be as redundant as transplanting field flowers into my kitchen garden. All we have to do to partake of beauty is gaze around ... past the scrap heap, that is.

APOSTROPHE XIV

Just Neighborly

It's a white clapboard farmhouse with a creek at its feet, and lilacs and rosebushes tumbling over the patched and picket fences. Around the barn, fat chickens mingle with ducks, pigs root under the noses of complacent cows. Twin giants of poplar trees shelter the footworn stoop. When my city eyes first took it in, it seemed a fairy tale farm. In my country years since, it has become an oasis of warmth and serenity, a touchstone of rural perfection, just a piece down the road from our postbox. It is the home of our former landlady and our nearest neighbor.

If you walked a straight line from our house to hers, it would measure but a bit over a mile. But you can't walk it straight. There are woods and thickets to circle, and a creek to cross, tumbled with sunwarm boulders for sitting and listening. After that, there's the hill to climb, and below it, a hollow furnished with wild rose brambles and crabbed apple trees.

We don't visit much. We both get busy with chores, and days, weeks pass without our noticing. She has new calves to tend, and our goats are due to kid, or the spring-house needs mending. But it's good to know, between us, that we're each there.

It's spring now, and the next time we go by, her tulips will be coming up. I'll tell her about my crocuses and the first woods buttercup I found. And that Dicey, the grey hen, is poorly. She'll know what to do.

Because there's a fat hill in the way, we can't see her place from our mountain, but sometimes we chat on the phone in winter, compare how deep our snows are and whether our pipes froze, or who heard coyotes on which night, and how close they sounded. Nothing newsworthy or world-shaking, just neighborly, which is best of all.

It's a world from the city, where we shared our neighbors' music and entertainments, their battles and the very smells of their cooking; where living so atop one another, we avoided human contact beyond a nod or a few words passed on the street. "Neighbor" means different things in different places. Our neighbor gives it fresh life.

I worry about her sometimes, though she'd hate it if she knew. She works so hard, alone with all the farm chores, has worked so long. At night, her parlor light is the last to go out in the valley; in the morning, her animals are the first to be paid mind. If her light ever fails to shine out over the farmyard, to catch the glint of the quivering poplar leaves, our mountain will feel the bereavment, our days won't be the same. It isn't the distance downmountain that matters. It's knowing, between us, we're there.

Strangers Are Persons, Too

Bedlam. It's the only way to describe those city years, years stitched with roomsful of chattering faces, and music, doorbells ringing, phones jangling, and meals as thronged and confused as boarding hotels'. Even those times we tried to get off to the wilds by ourselves, friends tagged along; a few were invited, but most just followed like prattling shadows. Everywhere. At home, I would shut the door on one assemblage at two in the morning, and find another trooping through the rooms shortly after breakfast.

Our absences did little to stem the tide, for we'd return from vacations to find romances being carried on in the back rooms, parties in the front, and notes stuffed under bottles of wine or empty coffee cups: "Thanks for the wine, here's some new," or, "Sorry we missed you, but we'll be back soon." Someone once left a sleeping bag in our yard, we'll never know who, and one day we came home to find a stained glass window propped on the front porch, a mysterious gift which almost made up for the scratches faceless others put on our records, the eternal post-picnic look of the kitchen. You'd have thought OPEN HOUSE was inscribed over our door.

Years on, when we moved to San Francisco, we swore closest friends to the secrecy of our new address and unlisted phone. We needed some time to ourselves, we explained, and wanted to explore unencumbered this mythic city. But it was no good. We were no sooner settled than the doorbell began ringing, the phone piercing all hours. And all this time, while one frantic part of me loved the fraternity, the involvement in others' lives, another yearned toward solitude, for a space of my own and the wholeness that might rest in seclusion.

Sometimes, these days, I think I might have carried that yearning too far. Among the benefits of this hillside was its very distance from people. While dearest friends could drive the long, roundabout miles for holiday visits and special festivities, it wasn't the sort of place one would, on a whim, drop in on, or bring by a sociable flask for an evening of sharing.

Weeks go by, in dim weathers, when we don't speak to a living soul. Oh, we'll wave from the postbox to the neighbor making her rounds, and sometimes the family who lives up the mountain now will honk as they grind past our meadow, and sometimes we'll drop by on the retired couple over past the town road. One or two valley neighbors phone now and then to ask about our mountain weather, and do we have any snow, or to tell us our postbox is near to overflowing. Their voices sound strange and distant, when we're used just to our own. It's a sort of dream state you get into in isolation, one Robinson Crusoe would well understand.

One of the county's elders tells us that once there were quite a few homesteads scattered over this mountain; she describes how their families used to visit by wagon and nag, and how the children got to school the same way, stopping to create simple mischief, like tying tree branches into circles on the course of their journeys. "You look for some grown-round limbs," she says. "They should still be there." I have looked, but I haven't found any. We have, though, stumbled across the bleached remains of log structures in woods clearings, and the midden mounds of old cellars, and up by the cattail pond, a garland of jonquils blooms each year, though there's not a scrap left of the home they once graced.

I have come to know the ghosts of our mountain better than most of the living beyond it, am firmer friends with its woods lodgers than with my scattered neighbors. If it weren't for Mike's presence—and for him, mine—I would probably grow cobwebbily weird, follow the way of the old recluse who long ago built our cabin. I've a growing feeling that he and I would get along just fine.

This solitude is neither a state we covet nor terribly mind. Acceptance of city strangers by a rural community, set in its comfortable ways, is at best measured. When the strangers are also outspoken and the holders of free-wheeling views, they may as well be Brobdingnagians.

Question: Why doesn't he cut his hair? Answer: He does, or rather, I do it for him, twice a year whether it needs it or not. Let grown in the winter, it serves as insulation.

Question: Why don't they take part in community doings? Answer: We don't enjoy pinochle, can't afford to sup at the tavern, disbelieve in rodeos, and are set to nodding by high-school sports.

Question: Just who do they think they are, anyhow? Answer: So far, we've settled on the following, which, though locally abrasive, are as best we can do: We are kin to the trees, which we see being cut for shortsighted profit, and to the wild creatures whose killing is summoned as sport; we are friends of the earth, which reels from man's chemical mayhem. We are not good Romans, doing what set-in-their-ways Romans do.

It doesn't necessarily follow that when the new landholder gets consumed by his farmy business, he drops his human concerns. Though the drummer is now at a distance, the beat is still heard. Swallowed up for five years by my monastic rounds, I was glad when, during the sixth, I was asked to write a weekly column for the two-county newspaper. My subjects forthwith included the look and feel of the seasons, the garden's enterprises, the sightings of flora and fauna . . . and in balance, my view of the monstrous risk of a nuclear plant proposed for this area's fringes, my abhorrence of a projected mobile home village for oldsters, the botch left by hunters in season, the civil rights of, yea, even gays, hippies, and, Lord help us, total *strangers*. Once I was invited to go back from whence I came, a resentful silence, sprinkled with handfuls of hate mail, settled over the land.

The *nerve*, just who do I think I am? Answer: A fellow trave-
ler, flawed as thee, concerned for the shape of the earthship
we share.

Years back, Mike and I camped out along the back roads of
Arizona. On one particularly dilapidated byway, two of our
tires blew. Towed into town, we asked the garage tender how
long it might take to replace them. He tilted his hat back and
looked at the lazy blue sky. "Can't say. Gotta send for 'em,
you know. Two, mebbe three days. We don't get in no hurry
around here." It took four. At the time, we thought such
languor maddeningly quaint. How nice to live where there's
no hurry, we told each other.

It is and it isn't. There are limits.

Before we bought our acreage, we inquired about the state
of the mile and a half ruin of road which wound uphill from
the nearest neighbor, bypassed our meadow bottom, and
connected with a graveled forest road at the hilltop. Oh, the
crew would fix it for us, we were assured. They did that for
all the neighbors. So we settled and waited. A good part of the
first year, and then the second, we were walled from the
world of postbox, neighbors, supplies for weeks on end by the
weather's designs on the untended byway. The third year,
we wrote the judge, asking politely if he might give it his attention. The judge replied that since it was not a county
road, it was out of his hands. In the weeks that followed, we
betook ourselves to the county records and proved to our satisfaction that it was indeed part of the county road system,
though long neglected. The D. A. argued it wasn't either.
Our lawyer opined it was. We laid out our proofs to the
judge and the county powers. Well, what if it is? they countered. Who said, even so, that they had to maintain it?
Through gritted teeth, we cited The Law, which by then we
could recite in our sleep. They pondered, they hemmed and

they hawed. Time passed, and wet weather threatened. The nice Judge made a call via the contested road (in a borrowed truck; his sedan couldn't make it), and suggested we purchase a horse. The nice Judge apologized for the delay. The nice Judge wrapped up the whole pestiferous package and sent it off to the State Attorney General. The A.G., bless his judicial soul, instructed the county in terms incontrovertible to obey the law: The road, the *county* road, must be brought up to standard and maintained thereunto. Amen.

One morning that October, the sounds of the rigs of the road crew greeted our ears. It was high, holy music.

Though "standard," even by local definition, is not quite what they brought it up to, we were in no mood to carp. Never mind a few rock piles, even the road to heaven is said to be marred. As long as they plowed it of deepest snows, we would rest content.

They didn't and don't. The snowplow which plies the wintered-in valley bypasses our junction as though it were a figment of some stranger's daydream. We wait; we are patient; we hate to complain. But now the three-year-old fix on the road is disintegrating, and we'll soon be as landlocked as in days of yore. If we return to beg recourse, the back fences will buzz. Just who do we think we *are*? Answer: Strangers.

It's axiomatic that the farther from centers of civilization, the more insular the inhabitants. Insularity, however, isn't necessarily wicked. Our neighbors, county-wide, seem content with their lot, and are, barring an occasional donnybrook whose outcome is seldom fatal, obliging toward one another. Sometimes, when I cause a fuss, which I seem to unaccountably often, I feel almost guilty of disturbing their somnolent peace. Sometimes I vow to keep my mouth shut, to limit my bumptious opinions to only Mike's ears, to confess to the goats my judgments of human folly. "A stranger's eye sees clearest" is unwelcome counsel in a strange land.

Each rural hamlet has its individual ambience, its own degree of indulgence and paranoia. When a stranger, especially if he's a city slicker, moves in, he is bound to be the butt of good-natured jape, as well as back fence tattle-tale. His long-term relationship to his neighbors is largely up to him. We opted for measured solitude. It is lonely, sometimes; we often hunger for familiar friends. The boon is that we can read all those books which sat idle in the hectic city, blast Beethoven over the meadow and jar not a soul, dance jigs on the rooftops with no one to call us mad. When such freedom pales, there are always our populous summers, when the meadow dust never settles for the traffic it bears.

"I was a stranger, and ye took me in." Matthew, XXV, 35

"I was a stranger, and ye took me not in." Matthew, XXV, 43

See there? Even Matthew waffled.

APOSTROPHE XV

No Horses

People who do often ask me why we don't have a horse, or a flock of them, or whatever grouping it is horses come in. ("Pride" would be good, but it's already taken.) Given our isolation, our ample acreage, and the fact that motorized transport is limited in heavy weather, it would seem a reasonable alternative to have hooves upon which to rely. It's a pleasant theory, and makes for nice daydreams too, the two of us astride brindled nags, riding off into sunsets, just like in the old movies. Mornings begun by the cry, "Saddle up!" Evenings ended amid the smells of sweaty leather. Horses might also add to the sylvan quality of our woodsy environs, their graceful forms lording above the hill's slide, their manes rippling in errant zephyrs.

The most practical reason for this lack is the cost of equine provender. The price of a barn for their housing runs a close second. Our choice of domestic creatures—with the exception of canine and feline, which we seem to have no control over—must rest with what they provide in return for their care. But I must admit that even were we as rich as Croesus, I doubt we'd keep horses. Oh, I might adopt a pony or two for playmates and to feed treats of apples in return for a loving nuzzle, or maybe a superannuated nag with her teeth gone to seed, too old to nip or get uppity. But ride them? Not on your life. My own two legs do just fine, and I usually know where they're headed and at what pace. Therein lies a tale.

In my citified youth, I was packed off each summer to Girl's Camp, there to study woods lore, have Healthy Adventure, make a passing acquaintance with flora and fauna— and to learn to ride horses. The flora and fauna and woods lore I took to just fine. The Healthy Adventure took a back seat to my pining sorely for malt shops and the cute boy down the block. The horseback lessons were a disaster.

The first time I was introduced to my assigned saddled creature, I backed off in holy terror. He (she? Gender was the last thing on my mind) was at least ten feet tall, and his eyes had the look of hellfire. First off, I demanded a ladder. My companions, already mounted and looking dismayingly cool and collected, tittered up a storm. Shame conquering

fear, I allowed myself to be helped, clutching wildly for purchase, onto the saddle, but before I could be instructed in the
mastery of the rein, the behemoth beneath me took one look
over his shoulder, snorted a thunderous snort, and took off
like his tail was afire. Down the road, over a fence, directly
under low branching trees. My howls for salvation did little
to soothe him. Clutching fistfuls of his mane for dear life, I
uttered my final Hail Mary's and whimpered to no one I was
too young and tender to die. In the middle of my umpteenth
Hail Mary, Mother of God, the crazed beast came to a dust-
rising halt a few feet in front of his stable quarter. As I remember, he turned his head toward his lathered backside,
curled his spittled lip and guffawed. As I collected my shat-
tered wits, the excursion's leader arrived at my side. Below
his flushed face, his belt was near to busting. The turncoat
cretin was laughing!

The following year at camp, when it befell time for the
horseback tomfoolery, I begged to be given a slow, plodding
creature, a reject maybe, who had never gotten the hang of a
gallop or goal. The leader grinned knowingly, and brought
before me a hoary nag. Her (this time, there was no mistaking) eyes were so rheumy, her back so swayed she could
have been Boanerges' great-grandmother. This was more
like it. Reassured, I reached out and patted her rump. She
almost fell down. I was helped, with hardly a shudder, into
the saddle. She breathed a heavy sigh, and together we
watched our ambitious companions ride off out of sight. Old
Nell didn't budge. I wasn't even sure she was still breathing,
which to my thinking, was just as well.

It was a pleasant hour, the two of us there in the sunlight.
After a while, I ventured a bit of conversation. Her ears
perked a bit, and she even amassed the energy to nod her
head. By the time the smug rough riders returned, we had

enough empathy established between us to ignore together their howls of derision. "The last shall be first," I whispered to Nell. Her ribs heaved a grateful reply.

That was my last stint at summer camp. Even my determined family couldn't tolerate my plunge into hysteria when the subject of further Healthy Adventure was broached. To assure my salubrity, they bought me a bicycle, which was blessedly close to the ground.

No, I wasn't cut out to be a horseperson. Oh, I like their genre all right, love to talk to them, rub their noble foreheads, look into their intelligent eyes. The nicer among them remind me of my gentle goats, a fact which fails to endear me to their keepers. It's just that I don't care to demean them or my person by mounting them, much less demanding of them transportation. And I'd appreciate it if those toddlers in our neck of the woods would stop galloping by, looking for all the world as though being born to the saddle were natural to human nature. It makes a person feel tacky, to eat their dust, makes her aware of the fun she's been missing all those years spent over wheels and pavement and a poor imitation of horsepower.

Thou Beside Me
in the Wilderness

A young writer dropped onto our doorstep last winter, announcing he'd been sent by a worthy magazine to do us up in an article. Urbane city couple turned subsistence farmers, that sort of thing. After we'd scraped the mud from his boots, hung his garments to dry and revived him with coffee, he settled down, recorder poised, and looked around. It was a dark, bitter day, and little light filtered in the cabin's windows. The parlor looked shrunken and dim, the kitchen was tracked with mud. Before the interview could begin, the goats bounded onto the porch to escape a snow flurry, and a ruckus rose from the yard where a testy dog chased a chicken. I ran out to scold her, while Mike drove the goats to the barn. He returned, rubbing fingers turned blue.

"Damn barn water's frozen again," he said.

"And Punkin's paw is bleeding from running on ice," I grumbled. "By the way, did you move that grain down to the feed bin?"

"Gawd, I forgot. Can't it wait 'til tomorrow?"

"My poor chickens will starve!"

The writer glanced at his recorder and cleared his throat. "Sorry," Mike said. "Okay, what's your first question?"

Click, went the recorder. "When are you going to get a divorce?"

By the time he left, hours later, I doubt he was any further assured of our wedded stability. Isolation brings out honesty, and we don't hide our skeletons well. But we had told him in truth that we had, even in the bowels of February, never considered division.

If a doubting partner ever cares to put his or her relationship to the ultimate test, let him move with his mate to the country . . . solitarily, with no communal distractions or familial supports. As lifeboats are to shipwreck survivors, rural solitude is to two human beings dropped together into an alien land with a new world of responsibilities. For the rurally bent, vows might better read, "In sickness and health, in drudgery and isolation." Marriages made in heaven can be broken on the division of chores, on twenty-four hour a day, three hundred sixty five days a year cheek-by-jowl togetherness.

If you think you know the very core of your selfhood, and are tolerably familiar with that of your mate . . . wait. Long winter nights, an endless span of look-alike winter days, farm demands and constraints, will unearth quirks and quiddities you had had no idea existed. They are likely to create even more. We have seen the lightest of hearts go forlorn with farm hardship, have witnessed apparently responsible people withdraw into their sheltering psyches and simply vegetate. Our competitive, group-centered society does little to nurture self-starters, recluses, abjurers. (Even Thoreau's ascetic friends thought him mad.) When two people are called on to become these together, in quite equal proportion, their guardian angels have to back off and cross their fingers.

Yet once a couple has agreed in honest unison that the rustic life is its goal, at least half the battle is gained. If one-

half of a twosome, however, hankers after a few pastoral
acres at the sacrifice of urban comforts, while the other has
a slew of misgivings, the burning of city bridges might court
catastrophe. It took but a single summer to convince one
couple we knew that they weren't ready for farming. Eight
months drove another two stir-crazy. A third, newly mar-
ried, made it through two years before, one burdened day,
the wife grabbed the rifle and riddled every object in sight.
(A lone goat was caught in the fray. The flighty chickens
took to the trees, and are probably huddled there to this day.)

Why, then, have we two survived thus far, our psyches
and affections intact? It's not easy, from dead center, to say.
Mike harbors a theory that one's enjoyment of a country
life-style lies in direct proportion to the harrassment one tolerated in the concrete jungle. Because he had supported a
family since he was eighteen, the free option of penury is a
blessing. Because he fought his way up the corporate ladder,
having to answer to no one but simple farm creatures is
measureless joy. Once driven to ulcer-breeding distraction by
business affairs, his tolerance of isolation is boundless, and
long beholden to office bureaucracy, his rural patience is that
of a profane saint.

An often-pampered, socially tutored urbanite, I am not so
easily pleased. The locals don't understand my outrageous
lingo? Strange, it once held my students in thrall. The
honchos don't cotton to my civil causes? My secretary once
smoothed the most radical of my righteous fits. The power
goes out, and I stomp about, ranting. How in the hell can I
finish typing this essay? We can't reach the postbox for days,
and I know with all that's in me that there's an assignment
therein, or a check that will cover the feed or the seeds or
whatever my latest indulgence. When I used to end up at odds
in the city, there was Magnin's to soothe my spirit, or a

bookstore to browse and select from, or an equally at-odds companion to mourn with in some espresso-scented cafe. Here on our at-odds mountain, Mike breeds his saintly patience, and counsels I do the same. Would you rather be in the city, he teases unbearably. Remember the traffic, the fumes, the doorbell always jangling, the business associates demanding to be entertained?

No, I wouldn't rather, not on my halcyon life; but oh, if there were just one musty, stack-spilling bookstore within miles, one ice cream parlor, even, with a tongue-stunning menu and small sticky tables full of fellow pistachio lovers.

The big sacrifices—funds, fashions, heart-to-heart friends—are easy. You face them and feel them and fill them with big exchanges. It's the trifles that tend to niggle and detain one's holy ways. Mike needs a new belt sander for his knife crafting, and the nearest is five hours away. I mail-order a few Christmas treasures for grandchildren in early October, and half of them fail to arrive 'til the season's long past. The tavern that buys the bulk of his apple-smoked cheese closes, and there are no others about to take up the slack, and oh woe, there go his tobacco and beer funds. He tries to make a vital long distance call, but the neighbors are on the four-party line endlessly discussing crops. (All praise, it used to be an eight-party.) The tarp over the hay springs a leak and the dearly bought bales turn moldy, and there won't be any more buyable until summer. I use a quote in an essay, but can't remember its author, and there's no one to call who might know. (It was Donne, dummy, and your mind, so unfed, is turning to jello.) The borrow of a cup of flour is only a fat mile away. Markets, the arts, and amity are an infinity.

We have read of a few social scientists who plunk human guinea pigs together in lab-like caves for a study of human behavior under trying conditions. I would offer for their consideration the lab of our mountain farm. In the absence of social stimuli, our minds do not atrophy, but hunger, rather, and bound. Contention and testiness constitute but a fraction of the means we employ to hold boredom and mind-rot at bay, and many is the winter morning when, having read until dawn, one of us will offer a new scientific discovery or a political quandary for debate. If the lifeboat we cohabit were ever to founder, we would no doubt prattle over some new revelation until the waters swept our words away.

Few people are given the chance to share each turn of every day. Fewer would probably care to. Friends, cherished belligerents and fellow confessors, we do. On long winter nights, we sit by the stove, Mike sipping his wine, I my tea, and confide our building frustrations. "Maybe we can find a farm-sitter in the spring and take a vacation," one of us offers. "Maybe you could go to Portland and buy that sander, and I could spend a few days at Penny's." Maybe. Before the goats freshen, after I've planted the greenhouse, if I sell this essay, or Mike that set of knives. But then the greenhouse will need refreshment, and the goats might contract bag fever, and any spare money really should go toward a new load of hay.

Then spring arrives, with its greening, blooming, and who could leave the apple blossoms in their full glory, and how sad it would be to miss the first asparagus shoots, and the wild geese are due any day.

Summer comes, with its friends on vacation. "Let us take over," they say. "You two get away." But this is the only time of the year we can share their company, and the bright days so welcome kinship and festivity, and would they really remember to tend my puny begonia, and that Sable needs an extra handful of creep on her grain if she's to behave during milking? Autumn, and the visitors dwindle, and the trees and skies turn to flame. A pleasant and peaceable season; we glean and store the harvest, rebuild the woodpile, snug the farm corners for winter's inevitability. Sullen days and long nights hover, and the earth-weighted silence. We have each other, we'll keep the haunts at bay. And some time in late January, one or the other of us will notice a mood, an absence of laughter, and we'll sit down with wine and tea and confide our frustrations. Plans will be made, familiar dreams pulled out and polished. Most important, we will listen, each to the other. No matter that the woes are familiar or futile, they are aired and disburdened; shared.

The confiding of feelings, though not easy for two private people, is often more managable than the down-to-earth sharing of chores. There is, on a man/woman farm, no room for role playing. If she rises first, to milk and let the chickens out, he out of kindness, as well as for the sake of efficiency, can have breakfast ready on her return. If he's busy chopping wood, she can sack the grain. Admittedly, the woman is at some physical disadvantage. Try as I might, I cannot lift 100-pound sacks of grain, though I'm working on it, and the heaviest chain saw is beyond my means. (That I don't take to the smaller one either has nothing to do with my sinew; my impatient attacks with the thing turn wood into matchsticks.) When a sex-crazed billy goat mounts me, I want strong-shouldered Mike nearby for a rescue. When I disappear into a snowdrift, I welcome a six-foot lifesaver.

We never discussed, even in the beginning, a proper division of labor. We did what was needed and what we liked best, and things fell to a natural order. He tills the garden, I mind it. I manage the chickens, he slaughters and cooks them. He chops the wood, I tote it indoors and keep the fires. Unless I'm bound to a writing deadline, we take turns with

the goat-milking and barn housekeeping. When my cooking palls, he dons the chef's hat, and our palates are the better for it. The major missions, like assisting at birthings or winter wood gathering, we share. We wouldn't think of missing the greeting of new life together, or tramping the forest haunts solitarily for Platonic ideals of downed trees.

It is only when the most practical, mechanical chore calls for cooperation that we get into trouble, for though my flesh might be willing, my distraction threshold is famously below sea level.

"Okay, now, hold that end of the board just so, and stay out of the blade's way."

I hold, just so. The saw whines at my side. "Oh, look, Mike, is that a hawk or an eagle?" The board bows, Mike turns off the saw and beats his brow.

"Dammit, pay attention, or we'll both end up paraplegics!"

"Sorry. It had white tips on its wings. I wonder. . . ."

"Joanie!"

Or, "Hold the ladder steady, now. I'm climbing clear to the top."

"Okay. Hey, the first hollyhock's blooming. See, the pink one there. . . ."

"Steady, I said!"

"Sorry. Woops, my shoe is untied, just a sec. . . ." I can quote no further. It is not pleasant to hear.

Mike once slipped from my unsteady ladder hold and tore open his palm during flight. I had to drive him fifty miles to the clinic to have the cut patched. My guilt knew no bounds, and though he was awfully decent about it, I vowed on the Good Book to do better. But can a woman whose younger-day hands were constantly smacked with rulers for classroom daydreaming grow into a handyman's helpmeet? The prognosis does not bode sanguine. The world is so full of a number of things, I am sure we should all be bewildered. Mike is, often, by me. It is a poor joke now, my inattention, like most of our foibles and failures. If I can manage to keep him in one comely piece, we'll muddle through. Together.

Do we battle? And how! Not often, never dirtily, but in prose and decibel worthy of melodrama. One of the bonuses of living out of anyone's earshot is the freedom to yell, slam doors in high dudgeon, and make your point, if need be, until dawn. The difference between city combat and country contention lies in both volume and subject. Though we can no longer lock horns over spendthriftiness or social misbehavior, this does not leave us wanting of subject. The slaughter of chickens, for example. How many? Which, if, and whether to breed both goats at the same time. Why I have to move his favorite chair gets us off to a rousing start. Why he has to fuss so about the crookedness of my garden rows is a perennial. I feed the animals too much, he is too chary; I don't discipline them, he is overly stern. The arguments sprinkle the seasons, add spice to a dismal span. Once we are purged of the volatile passions, we return to our rounds none the worse for their letting and eager to revert to our easy intimacy. There's world enough out there of confusion and hostility; our mountain absorbs the small storms and binds us in large harmony.

In silence and isolation, I have found a self I never suspected. Thrown together on this inland island, we find, over time, one another. I can think of few worthier purposes than for two fond and flawed human beings to explore themselves and each other to the very soul's fabric. "The Book of Life begins with a man and a woman in a garden. It ends with Revelation."*

So be it, and our dual destiny.

APOSTROPHE XVI

My Gypsy Wagon

By the tail end of summer, I am ready to get my gypsy wagon together and traipse off to the islands. Which islands, I'm not yet certain. It's just that "islands" sounds more exotically distant than, say, the mountains, which I'm already in, or a sunbelt I know by heart, or even a cultural Baalbek such as the hundred mile distant town of Hermiston, which place

---

* A Woman of No Importance, Oscar Wilde.

I hoard for the big game. The gypsy wagon too is still a figment of my post-summer dreams. But oh, what a structure it
is in my imagination: a prairie schooner sort of affair, set
high on painted wheels, roofed with rainbow-hued rags and
frayed patchwork, and sporting all manner of worn pots and
implements hung rattletrap from its wooden beams. The
traveling home will have room, of course, for a number of
goats, dogs, cats and a few chickens and ducks for wayfaring
companions. If he promises to cook and tinker, I can even
make room for Mike.

The circumstance which invariably breeds this yearning
is the last round of city visitors who ply up our hill before diminishing daylight and autumn frosts send them packing
to more temperate climes. To many of them, too darn many,
our homely aerie is but a branch to light on amid their world
wanderings. For a homebody who has not yet seen Hermiston, their gadding-about is almost too much to bear.

This year, early on, there was John, just back from a flight
to New York. Before he left, the Aronsons dropped by to
share tales of their recent adventures throughout Appalachia.
Pete spent the following span of days here, recovering from
a tour of Western Europe. (Paris was humid and too crowded,
he dared complain.) He didn't get much chance to relate the
tour's highlights, because Lisa, his new lady companion (the
old one having left to take up weaving in Denmark), was full
of accounts of her recent meander through Tibet and Nepal.

There was a week between there, after they left, for a return to earth, for reshaping the habit of farm chores and daydreaming rounds; for staring past the familiar mountains,
and envisioning roads tending toward shining towers, and
Eylsiums greenly unsullied. Then it was August, and the
maps were brought out again, now to trace Elsie's route to our
hill by way of Hawaii. Luce, sad to say, couldn't come with

her this year. He and Mark opted for a trip to Rome. They might visit later, they promised, to recount the look of that part of the world, maybe bring us a hunk of provolone and a flask of house Chianti. (I will stash the foreign treasures in my gypsy wagon for a feast under foreign stars.)

How do they do it, these voyagers? The wonder is enough to make a homebody crawl up the wall. I mean, what with the goats and the flocks and the gardens, and the winter wood-pile's demands, I can't even make it to Hermiston, a modest hundred miles off. It's not, mind you, that I don't cherish my own south and north forty, nor even that I don't prefer such repartee as our feathered and furred creatures offer to con-versations with nabobs and kings. It's just that the world seems so beautiful and new when you haven't yet seen but a smidgen, and when travel is confined to hauling in hay and grain for the equally sheltered creatures. Our journeying friends tell me it's not, really; they pat my straw-tangled head and assure me how lucky I am, that home is the best place of all, and how they wish they could trade adventures. I look out my window, past the pear thicket and old apple orchard, past the mountains that embrace the valley I know by heart now, and feel the truth of their consolations. What would a day be without my roosters' alarm, the look of my morning meadow?

And yet . . . I'm not ready yet to dismantle that gypsy wagon built of ragged dreams, its painted wheels sturdy enough to take me beyond the meridian where the meadow road leads. The farm was dream too, and now from its height, I keep looking beyond the far mountains, wonder-ing. The goats nuzzle my arm, a chicken pecks at my toes, the ducks parade the green shadows. Mike calls me to give him a hand. Yes, it would have to be big enough for all of us, big enough for the whole home hillside.

From the Desperate City...

O nce upon some decades past, our church compelled my young classmates and me to enter an annual religious retreat. Rounded like docile lambs into a sanctuary, we were given sanctimonious tracts to contemplate and stern warnings to utter not a sound. To me, those three-day interludes were a vision of limbo. What was I supposed to *do* with all those empty hours, how could I possibly feel graced in such a verbal vacuum? By the time the ordeal was over, I was ready to tear into the nearest devilment at hand.

Between retreats and other grown-up inventions, my Grandmother often regaled me with stories of her stint in the wilds of Arizona, where her only neighbors were stoic Indians, and she saw no one but her youngsters and ailing mate for weeks at a time. How dreadful, I used to think, offering prayers that my adult fate held no such solitary travail.

And now, years beyond, here sits the grown child, mistress of a solitary retreat in the wilds of Oregon, doing the holy sisters and my stoic Grandmother proud. But they have long since shed their earthly concerns. It is the living who watch from a distance, those friends in the cities we fled, and visitors who, after a month sharing our country solitude, go testy and spirit-soured. From their urban menages, they write anxious letters, send Care packages of literature to feed our farmish heads, call long distance when we're silent for more than a season. Is everything all right, are we snowed in, depressed, about to cannibalize one another? Have the natives burned us at split-rail stakes or poisoned our springs, has the larder gone bare? No, no, we tell them, we're fine, we're happy (unless it's February), we're just, well, you could say in retreat.

They gave us, when we moved here, less than a year. Mike, the people-leader, bon vivant, the teller of tall tales in city taverns, would die of human deprivation, they surmised, and as for me, such a social butterfly would surely lose her wings and her direction. Why, I couldn't even grow a decent houseplant in my city prime, how could I hope to feed us on a downtrodden farm?

Seven years is a Biblical span. The major part of our building is done. We have learned pretty well how to hold off disaster and how to make this earth parcel thrive. We have "driven life into a corner" and flourished, and though a steep path lies ahead, we have reached a sheltering ledge where we can take a breath and look around. Far from what and where we were then, we measure what we have gained.

Writings about the boon of rustic simplicity have become common coin, their authors proclaiming the resultant health to the earth and its residents, the independence offered. The subject shouldn't be, as it often is, glossed over lightly, for within it lies the kernel of everyman's purpose. It is said that Western civilization, industrial, massive, and mindless of its human cogs, has moved at a velocity far beyond our rate of adjustment, that while we are still physically tuned to a pastoral pace, this society demands ever more rapid adaptation. Such a quandary might well account for our ailments and frustrations; it also drives a number of us to stop the machine's endless clatter and examine its function and purpose.

The option for subsistence farming is a selfish one, at bottom. It contributes to no one beyond the farmer himself, has little effect upon the GNP. Though it might salvage a patch of earth from a dozer for the time being, it is apt also to diminish further the shrinking amount of wild land. (Would *our* farm have fallen back into its natural state in fifty or a hundred years, or would some greedy land snapper-upper have been less protective of it than we?) If everyone were to take it into his head to transport to the country tomorrow, the remaining wilderness would give up its ghost of a chance for survival.

Luckily for the earth's sake, such a scenario is unlikely. The majority clings to its manmade labyrinths like a Minotaur in its lair. Few therein, I suspect, lead the lives of quiet desperation attributed to them. Monotonous, bland, stressful, perhaps, but desperation diminishes among a people well fed, comfortably housed, and distracted by every recreative invention.

Still, there are a few who want for more. We ourselves didn't care to get any richer. Bigger and better living quarters had lost their appeal, new cars were toys we could well do without. Our careers contributed little to the betterment of anyone's lot, and such civilized pleasures as art, music and a spate of entertainments seemed less and less worth the servitude required for their gain. Our basic needs, we reckoned, were like all of mankind's: shelter, an adequate diet, and the peace in which to enjoy our abundant human being. Never mind our earth-ship's fellow passengers, or mankind's driven sins, we had done our part and could now go into retreat, bounden only to a morsel of God's greensward and ourselves.

Selfish, yes, and there lies the dilemma. Adequacy and self-reliant survival are poor fare for those hungers beyond

gut and muscles' satiety. The tending of gardens and creatures, the structure of shelter, though worthy and gratifying
employments, do little to keep the synapses snapping, the
cortex nourished. Though a fool would make a poor farmer,
a drone, given dedication to the task, might do well. In isolation, no matter how pleasingly pastoral, the life of the mind is
eventually driven to feed on itself.

On a summer day, I come up from the green, scented garden and glance at a newspaper. Greenpeace is sailing thither
and yon to rescue the whales, Lilly is applying his dolphin
learning to the human psyche, the Peace Corps is returning
to life in the struggling third level world. Its headlines swallowed, the paper is set aside, for the beans must be snapped
and the peas shelled. Over busy fingers, my thoughts scat-

ter. I am my own peace corps person on a world level unmea-
sured. The goats' brains aren't so shabby that they can't expand mine, and who knows what struggling wild life we've
rescued in the shelter of this one-sixty? (But, oh to be out on
the embattled sea, watching for whales, to explore the dol-
phins' wise lingo; to share mine with a like-minded soul. . . .)
Winter, I riffle through a mountain of journals saved for just
such long nights. Ahh, see here, Acrosanti is thriving, and
this group is marching on nuclear plants for the sake of us
all, and here's a fellow establishing holistic centers throughout doctor-poor rural counties. A craft show in Portland
catches my eye, and a theatre benefit in Ashland. (I was good
with benefits once, long ago, and managed some worthy craft
shows in my time. How exhilarating it was, the accomplishment with and for others.) The fire gutters, more logs to
bring in, and we'd better go see that the barn water pipes
haven't frozen.

We have established as truth that isolation breeds self-
understanding, and the shape of new wisdoms, even. The
silent spaces for thought and review it engenders are priceless. Yet after a time, one yearns to share their textures and
apply their benificence to a cause beyond the limits of one's
acres. Simplicity is close to essential, but it is complexity that
nurtures the mind.

I just wish I didn't keep remembering that Thoreau stayed
at Walden for little more than a year, that while there he went
to Concord frequently; that there was brilliant Emerson when
he wanted for colloquy. How much more he might have to
teach me if he had stayed for seven, how much strength I
could borrow if he'd truly entered into isolation. Especially in
February. "From the desperate city you go into the desperate
country, and have to console yourself with the bravery of
minks and musk-rats." Fie, Henry David! I fare better with

the Bhagavad Gita, which at least takes my head beyond the rural predicament, and which gives no room to desperation in either quarter.

Mike, of solid New England stock, grows anxious when I bury my head for long periods in exotic philosophies. He comes in from his down-to-earth labors and finds the rooms wafted with incense, and me sitting cross-legged on the floor.

"O-o-om," I hum, unaware of his intrusion.

"Excuse me, did you hide the small hammer somewhere?"

"O-o-o-m, shh."

"Joanie. . . ?"

"Mike, how can I possibly enter into another state if you keep interrupting?"

"Sorry, but I can't find the damned hammer. Besides, I'd rather you stayed here."

"I *am* here. I'm just trying to be aware of my hereness."

He shakes his head and returns to his labors, a worried look on his face. Thoreau and the New England Transcendentalists are fine, but when I immerse myself in the realms of Ram Dass and Meher Baba, he feels alienated, fears the mountain is making me weird. I don't dare tell him I'm thinking of hanging prayer wheels around the cabin quarter. "I went to the woods . . . to front only the essential facts of life." Thoreau and Baba aren't that far apart. Self-imposed exile does strange things to people, but with Mike as my buoy, I won't drift too far. (But, oh, I will build me a teahouse in the hushful wood and there meditate for lost hours, unaware of cockcrow and bleat calling me to my chores. My unearthly excursions will be both reward and punishment for this chosen forswearing.)

There exists no solid demarcation between isolation and desolation, just as there is no perfect balance between being crowd-maddened and downwind from nobody. We have